FINANCE
AND
ACCOUNTING

FOR
GENERAL MANAGERS
Second Edition

*a practical guide
to reading and understanding
financial reports*

HENRY H. BEAM

Western Michigan University

KENDALL/HUNT PUBLISHING COMPANY
4050 Westmark Drive Dubuque, Iowa 52002

CONTENTS

PREFACE TO SECOND EDITION

Since I wrote the first edition of this book in 1990, it has become increasingly difficult to read and understand financial statements. In its attempt to have financial reports more accurately reflect a firm's assets and its obligations at a point in time, the accounting profession has also made it more difficult to read financial statements. More than once while preparing the second edition I have had to ask my colleagues in Accountancy to explain a particular entry to me, such as Deferred Tax Assets or LIFO Reserve. My intent in this edition, as in the first, is to help general managers read financial reports such as the Annual Report prepared by all publicly held corporations.

The second edition also includes a new chapter on exchange rates, an increasingly important topic as more American companies, large and small, do business abroad.

Over the past five years, corporate executives, small business owners and students have told me how *Finance and Accounting for General Managers* helped them really understand financial statements for the first time. They especially commented on the usefulness of my "geometric approach" to understanding entries on the balance sheet. I appreciate their compliments, and hope the second edition will make it even easier to read and understand financial reports.

Henry H. Beam

PREFACE

Can you look at a firm's balance sheet and assess its financial health with confidence in less than five minutes? If not, then this book was written for you. In reality, managers as well as business school students have a great deal of difficulty reading and understanding basic financial reports such as the balance sheet and income statement, even if they have taken one or more courses in accounting or finance. Yet financial reports are an integral part of business life, and the manager who doesn't know how to read them is at a severe disadvantage.

I use a geometric approach to explain the balance sheet and the income statement which does not require any prior knowledge of bookkeeping or accounting. Since the book's focus is entirely on how to understand financial reports, there's no need to spend time explaining how to make those entries. That's the job of the bookkeeper and the accountant. General managers need to be able to read and understand financial reports, not prepare them.

Chapter 1 introduces the geometric representation of the balance sheet. Depreciation, cash flow and taxes are covered in Chapter 2. Chapter 3 explains how to compute and use nine financial ratios to quickly and accurately assess a firm's financial health. A form is provided to facilitate this analysis.

Chapter 4 explains the often confusing differences between the cash method, the modified cash method and the accrual method of accounting. It tells why small businesses usually use the modified cash method and large businesses the accrual method. Chapters 5, 6 and 7 cover leverage (the use of debt in the firm's capital structure), valuation of a business, and contribution analysis (which tells how to find where a business makes most of its money). The final two chapters cover breakeven analysis, payback period and an introduction to discounted cash flow techniques and the time value of money.

Students frequently comment that my approach has helped them really understand for the first time how to evaluate a firm's income statement and balance sheet. General managers and small business owners also should find this book useful. It will help them deal knowledgeably with the specialists in accounting and finance with whom they must work.

I owe a particular debt of gratitude to Tom Carey, my colleague in the Department of Management, for his help and encouragement in writing a book about finance and accounting that managers and students alike could understand. A special word of thanks goes to the many students who have provided helpful suggestions for this book. Their input is always welcome.

Henry H. Beam

INTRODUCTION

This book was written for general managers or generalists, as they are often called, especially those with little or no formal training in accounting or finance. Its purpose is to provide them with enough understanding of the basic concepts of finance and accounting to ask meaningful questions of the specialists in those areas with whom they will work.

The need for a book like this became evident to me from my experiences teaching courses in strategic management. Many students exhibited excellent technical skills in accounting and finance. However, when asked to assume the role of a general manager, only a few could actually understand what the financial data presented in annual reports or cases studied in class actually meant. This book seeks to remedy this situation by presenting accounting and finance from the point of view of the general manager (the *consumer* of financial data) rather than the functional specialist (the *preparer* of it).

The accounting and financial statements we take for granted in business today are actually rather recent developments. Double entry bookkeeping, first summarized by the Italian monk Fra Luca Pacioli in 1494 in his book *Summa de Arithmetica Geometria Proportioni et Proportionalita*, was one of the major steps forward in the commercial development of the Western world. It made it possible to tell at a glance the profit or loss that had occurred for a given period of time (month, year, voyage) and the related assets, liabilities and net worth. It also made it possible to calculate a rate of return on the funds invested in the venture.

The second major development occurred in 1913 with the passage of the legislation enacting a federal tax on the income of corporations and individuals. Initially levied at 1%, it soon rose during World War I to a level of 12%. By the time World War II ended in 1945, it was near the 50% level, where it stayed with minor adjustments for forty years. Then the Tax Reform Act of 1986 made significant reductions in taxes for both corporations and individuals. Today a major source of business for the accounting profession is the determination (and minimization) of taxes for both corporations and individuals. As we'll see in Chapter 2, taxes are what make the concepts of depreciation and cash flow so important in business.

Another important aspect of accounting, one that we will not deal with but from which we will benefit greatly, is auditing. The purpose of auditing is to verify the integrity of the underlying data on which accounting statements are based. In the United States we are particularly fortunate that we can have a high degree of confidence in financial statements which have been audited and approved by a certified public accounting firm. Managers can rely on the data presented to them to be accurate. However, the general manager remains fully responsible for knowing what the data presented means, and that requires an understanding of the concepts of accounting and finance. This book attempts to present the most important of these concepts in a clear, concise manner starting with a geometric representation of the balance sheet in Chapter 1.

CONCEPTS OF ACCOUNTING 1

The basic concepts of accounting are developed here in a simple, straightforward fashion that requires no prior knowledge of accounting. Often accounting courses require so much detail work to get statements to balance that students fail to see the forest for the trees. Thus while most students learn how to *prepare* financial statements correctly in their accounting courses, far too few know how to *interpret* them once they have been prepared. Hence we will concentrate on understanding *what* has been presented and leave the technical details of *how* it should be prepared to the accountants.

Two financial statements are of primary interest to the general manager: the balance sheet and the income (or profit and loss) statement. Each serves a distinctive purpose. The balance sheet is a snapshot of the firm's financial *position* at a particular instant in time. The income statement is a summary of a firm's financial *transactions* for a given period of time. Taken together they present a reasonably accurate picture of a firm's financial condition and performance over time when interpreted by a manager who knows how to read them.[1] This book will show you how to both read and interpret these two very important statements.

THE BALANCE SHEET

The balance sheet is constructed using the fundamental rule of accounting:

Assets = Liabilities + Shareholders' Equity

By definition, this equation is always true. If for some reason the equality relationship does not hold, then a mistake has been made in one of the categories (assets, liabilities, or shareholders' equity). This relationship is so important that it should be memorized for recall at a moment's notice.

We can more clearly understand this concept by visualizing the balance sheet in geometric terms. Consider the balance sheet to be a rectangle divided into two equal parts by a vertical line, as shown in Exhibit 1.1. The left half represents assets, the right half liabilities plus shareholders' equity. From the definition that assets always equal liabilities plus shareholders' equity, we know the two halves must always be equal in size. This means that any time we make an entry that changes the size of one side of the rectangle, a corresponding entry (or entries) must be made in the other side to keep the sizes equal.

---

1. Accountants, bankers and financial analysts also place considerable importance on the statement of changes in financial position (formerly the funds statement), but this is of less practical use to most general managers than the income statement and the balance sheet and will not be discussed. Accounting Principles Board Opinion No. 19 issued in 1971 makes this a required statement in annual reports along with the balance sheet and the income statement.

Assets	Liabilities + Shareholders' Equity
1/2 Total Area	1/2 Total area

Exhibit 1.1. Geometric representation of the balance sheet.

The Asset Half

Accountants provide a marvelous service for busy managers by listing assets from most to least liquid. Liquidity refers to the ease with which an asset can be turned into cash, which by definition is the most liquid asset. Thus simply by looking at the location of an asset, we know the accountant's appraisal of the ease or difficulty of turning it into cash. Whenever cash is spent for an asset, the cash category is reduced and an equal amount added to the asset category for which that cash was spent. Similarly, if an asset is sold, the cash slice is increased by the amount received for the asset and the asset category is reduced by that amount, but the total area of the asset half remains unchanged.

The Other Half

This half represents claims on assets. It is divided into two parts: liabilities (creditors' claims) and shareholders' equity (owners' claims). Liabilities are listed first in order of expected payment, the most current obligations coming first. Liabilities are further divided into two major categories: short term (due in less than a year, including current portion of long term debt) and long term (due after a year).

Shareholders' equity has traditionally consisted of three entries:[2]

1. Capital contributed. The amount received for sale of stock at par value.
2. Capital in excess of par. The amount, if any, received in excess of the par value of the stock when it was sold.
3. Retained earnings. The accumulated earnings (or losses) after taxes which have been retained in the business rather than returned to shareholders in the form of dividends. This figure should be positive, reflecting accumulated earnings greater than losses, but may be negative, reflecting accumulated losses greater than earnings.

---

2. Starting in 1982 another entry may appear in the shareholders' equity account of firms doing a significant amount of business abroad. This entry summarizes gains or losses which would arise due to fluctuations in exchange rates if the amounts earned in a foreign country in that country's currency were translated into dollars. Since the amounts earned in a foreign country are typically reinvested in that country, no actual translation from that country's currency (marks, pounds, yen) into dollars is actually made. Hence the entry is called something similar to "unrealized gains or losses due to translating foreign currencies into dollars." Prior to 1982 unrealized gains or losses due to foreign currency translations had been accounted for on the income statement rather than the balance sheet, a practice that sometimes led to widely fluctuating earnings reports from year to year. Unless a firm does a sizable percentage of its business in foreign countries (e.g., 25% or more), this account can generally be ignored since it will be small compared to retained earnings. The unrealized foreign currency gains and losses account should show a pattern of losses and gains as currency exchange rates change, and hence should tend to fluctuate around zero. Accounting for translation of foreign currency transactions is covered by Financial Accounting Standards Board (FASB) Statement No. 8.

Be careful not to make the mistake of thinking that retained earnings is like a bank account with cash in it that can be spent as management sees fit. Management can't "spend" retained earnings because retained earnings is a claim on assets, not a bank account with cash in it. Cash and all items that can be turned into cash are always listed on the Asset (left hand) side of the balance sheet. Retained earnings is a component of shareholders' equity, which shows how much of a firm's assets (valued in dollars) can be claimed by shareholders after all liabilities, short and long term, have been paid off.

THE SIMPLEST BALANCE SHEET

Now consider the development of the simplest balance sheet, that of a new firm, the XYZ company, whose only transaction so far has been to sell stock for cash. If 100,000 shares of stock are sold at $10 per share (assuming no brokerage fee to sell the stock and par value of $10 per share), the firm will have one asset (cash, $1,000,000), no liabilities and shareholders' equity in the form of capital contributed of $1,000,000. This initial situation is represented both geometrically and in traditional accounting fashion in Exhibit 1.2.

If every obligation (e.g., payroll, materials, new equipment) were paid the instant it was incurred, we would never have any liabilities.

Geometric Representation

Assets	Liabilities + Shareholders' Equity
Cash $1,000,000	Capital contributed, $10 par value $1,000,000

Accounting Representation

Assets		Liabilities + Shareholders' Equity	
Cash	$1,000,000	Liabilities	$_____0
		Capital contributed	$1,000,000
		Retained earnings	_____0
	_____	Shareholders' equity	$1,000,000
Assets	$1,000,000	Liabilities + Shareholders' equity	$1,000,000

Exhibit 1.2. Geometric and traditional accounting representauon after sale of 1 00,000 shares of stock at $1 0 per share.

But such is rarely the case. When we add an asset we have not yet paid for (which is not unusual; most firms give thirty days to pay, sometimes longer) we add an equal amount to the liabilities block.

There is nothing inherently wrong with incurring liabilities unless, as we shall see, they get too large for our ability to pay them. Indeed, one of the important skills a manager should develop is the ability to know when a firm has reached the point where it has trouble paying its bills. This is a bad sign, just as it is when an individual cannot pay his or her own bills.

Some typical transactions are summarized in Exhibit 1.3 to show their effect on the rectangles. Remember, after every transaction, Assets must equal Liabilities plus Shareholders' equity. If they don't, then an error has been made somewhere in accounting for the transaction. Note that after each of these transactions the size of the two halves is always equal, although in the third transaction the size of each half decreases and in the fourth and fifth transactions the size of each half increases. Also note the power of double entry bookkeeping: although simple in format, it is flexible enough to handle any transaction, whether it be a small one for a local storekeeper or a multi-million dollar one for General Motors.

Now we will consider what an "ideal" balance sheet should looklike: how big should each major account be with respect to the other accounts? Certainly a good balance sheet will differ by industry and by size of firm, but it is helpful to have a single, general standard as a point of departure. Students often want to compare a particular ratio for a company to the industry norm to see if there is a significant deviation from it. This procedure can indeed be helpful, particularly for firms in unfamiliar industries. However, it is a poor substitute for developing the skill to *sense* when a ratio is out of line *without* having to look it up in a table of industry norms.

Transaction	Assets Account/Amount		=	Liabilities Account/Amount		+	Share-holders' Equity Amount
1	1,000 machine bought for cash	Cash Machine	−1,000 +1,000		–0–		–0–
2	1,000 machine bought on account	Machine	+1,000	Accounts payable	+1,000		–0–
3	Depreciation of machine, 200	Machine	−200		–0–		−200
4	Borrow 1,000	Cash	+1,000	Debt	+1,000		–0–
5	Earn 1,000	Cash	+1,000		–0–		+1,000
6	Customer pays 500 on account	Cash Accounts receivable	+500 −500		–0–		–0–

Exhibit 1.3. Some typical accounting transactions (all figures in $).

Fortunately, a simple model of the ideal balance sheet is readily obtained. Simply split the total rectangle into equal quarters, then split the two top quarters in half again to give six basic categories, as shown in Exhibit 1.4. The following relationships, the basis of ratio analysis, are easily verified visually from this geometric representation:

Norm (% of total)	Assets	=	Liabilities + Shareholders' Equity	Norm (% of total)
25%	Liquid current assets		Current liabilities	25%
25%	Inventory		Long term debt	25%
50%	Fixed assets * land * plant * equipment		Shareholders' equity	50%
100% total				100% total

Exhibit 1.4. The six basic categories of a balance sheet.

1. *Long term assets equal shareholders' equity.* Indeed, long term assets can be considered financed by shareholders' equity. In other words, the money the shareholders originally paid for their stock, plus accumulated retained earnings (earnings that are not paid out in dividends but are retained for use in the business) has been used to purchase long term assets such as machines, land and buildings which are expected to have an economic life longer than a year.

2. *Short term assets equal total liabilities.* Theoretically if the firm were to go out of business tomorrow, it would be able to pay off its bills and repay short and long term debt with short term assets. That is, none of the long term assets would have to be sold to pay off short term liabilities.

3. *Current assets equal twice short term liabilities.* This provides a comfortable margin for paying off liabilities due within a year. This is often called the current ratio (current assets divided by current liabilities) and should be about 2: 1, which can be readily verified by looking at Exhibit 1.4.

4. *Liquid current assets (cash, cash equivalents and accounts receivable) equal short term liabilities.* This recognizes the fact that inventories (the other component of current assets) may be hard to sell for full value on short notice, and provides a measure of a firm's ability to pay its bills upon demand if need be. It is called the *liquidity ratio* (or sometimes the *acid test*) and, again looking at Exhibit 1.4 for visual confirmation, it has a normal value of 1: 1.

5. *Long term debt should be one-half of shareholders' equity or less.* This relationship strikes a balance between two often conflicting goals:

    a. Desire to expand. Some long term debt is desirable because it allows a firm, especially an asset intensive one, to expand more rapidly than it could using only internally generated funds.

    b. Caution. Too much long term debt is undesirable because the firm may not be able to make interest payments on all its debt if it operates at a loss, and consequently may find itself in default of a loan and headed into bankruptcy proceedings.

A maximum long term debt to equity ratio of 0.5 is a good compromise given these conflicting goals. This ratio is very useful because it can be used to estimate how much long term debt a firm can safely carry, or how much unused borrowing capacity it has. Thus if shareholders' equity were $100,000,000, the firm could expect to borrow up to $50,000,000 without difficulty if other aspects of its situation were normal. If it has already borrowed $30,000,000, then its unused long term debt capacity is estimated to be $20,000,000 ($50,000,000 – $30,000,000).

The following general relationships hold:

$$\text{Maximum long term debt capacity} = .5 \times \text{Shareholders' equity}$$

$$\text{Unused long term debt capacity} = .5 \times \text{Shareholders' equity} - \text{Present long term debt}$$

In general, total debt (short term plus long term) should not be larger than shareholders' equity.

By mentally envisioning the numbers on the balance sheet in the proportional form shown in Exhibit 1.4, a manager can quickly gain much insight into the financial condition of a firm. In particular he or she can learn to sense when one of the numbers is out of proportion and a possible sign of trouble. Note also that the relationships discussed above hold regardless of the size of the firm, attesting to the power of the double entry form of bookkeeping.[3] These basic balance sheet relationships will be considered further in Chapter 3 where we learn how to assess the financial health of a firm using ratio analysis.

THE INCOME STATEMENT

Managers and shareholders alike expect a business to earn a profit, which is usually called net income in the financial world. The income statement is the primary accounting report to summarize revenues earned and expenses incurred for a specific period of time. The most familiar period is one year (hence the phrase annual report), but interim statements are commonly published and mailed to shareholders every three, six and nine months as well. The terms *sales* and *revenues* are used interchangeably. The income statement is laid out in the format shown in Exhibit 1.5.

Revenues or sales are the dollar value of goods sold or services rendered for the period, less any returns or allowances for bad debts.[4] (There are three basic ways to account for revenues and expenses; these will be covered in Chapter 4.)

---

3. An alternative form of the balance sheet, called the position statement, lists current assets first, then subtracts current liabilities to obtain working capital. Other liabilities (e.g., long term debt) are then subtracted from working capital to obtain shareholders' equity, or the excess of assets over liabilities. The position statement format, once popular, is rarely used anymore.

4. A firm's accountants will determine the method of determining revenue to be used. Virtually all large firms are on what is called the accrual basis, meaning that revenues and expenses are counted when they occur, not necessarily when payment is received or made. Many small businesses are on a modified cash basis, meaning that revenues and expenses are counted when the payment is received or made, which could be in a different accounting period than when the service was rendered or received. These methods are explained further in Chapter 4.

XYZ Company Income Statement, 19XX	
Revenues (sales)	$XXX
–Expenses	–XXX
Operating (pre-tax) income	$XXX
– Income taxes	–XXX
Net income	$XXX

Exhibit 1.5. Format for income statement.

Expenses are the costs incurred to produce the revenue. The following are the most important expense items on the income statement:

1. *Cost of goods sold (CGS) or cost of sales.* This is what it cost to make the product or produce the service, and is generally about 75-80% of sales. Cost of goods sold is calculated as follows by type of firm:
   a. *Manufacturing firm.*
      Cost of goods sold = Beginning inventory + Purchases – Ending inventory
      Unless otherwise indicated, both beginning and ending inventory include work in process.
   b. *Retailing firm.*
      Cost of goods sold = Beginning inventory + Purchases – Ending inventory
   c. *Service firm.*
      Cost of goods sold = Cost of services provided
      In many service firms (e.g., hospitals, insurance agencies), cost of supplies is small in comparison to cost of services and there is effectively no inventory. Cost of services is primarily labor cost.
2. *Selling, general and administrative expenses (SG&A).* Often called overhead expenses, these items usually cannot be directly attributed to the manufacture of a specific product so they are accounted for separately.
3. *Research and development (R&D) cost.* R&D expenses are charged against revenues when they occur (expensed, in the accountant's terminology) because their extent, duration and ultimate value can rarely be accurately estimated.
4. *Interest.* The amount of interest paid, primarily on long term debt. If a firm has no long term debt, it may not have any interest charges. Interest charges are a deductible expense for purposes of computing taxes.
5. *Operating income.* The income before taxes, also called pre-tax income. Operating income may show adjustments for special or one-time income or expense items, such as gain on sale of a plant or loss on sale of outdated inventory.
6. *Income taxes.* These are computed according to the corporate and applicable state tax schedules in effect. It's the accountant's job to compute all the pertinent taxes. As a rule of thumb, for firms

with sales of a million dollars or more, total taxes (federal, state and local) will be about forty to fifty percent of operating income.

7. *Net income.* This is the "bottom line," what is left over for distribution to shareholders in the form of dividends, or reinvestment in the firm. Earnings per share is equal to net income divided by shares outstanding, and is the most widely watched measure of financial performance.

LINKING THE TWO STATEMENTS

Accounting can be considered an iterative process. The income statement (results for a period of time) represents the difference in entries on the beginning and ending balance sheets (statements of accounts at a point in time) for the period covered by the income statement. In particular the general manager should know that the change in shareholders' equity during the year is generally equal to net income less any dividends paid.

$$\begin{array}{llll} \text{Shareholders'} & - \text{Shareholders'} & = \text{Net income} & - \text{Dividends} \\ \text{equity, end} & \text{equity, start} & \text{for year} & \text{paid} \\ \text{of year} & \text{of year} & & \end{array}$$

This general relationship could be modified by special events during the year, such as sale or redemption of stock. [5]

SUMMARY

Taken together, the balance sheet and income statement provide a reasonably complete picture of a firm's financial condition and performance over time. The general manager should know how to read and understand both of these important accounting statements, but doesn't need to know how to prepare them. That's the accountant's task. In the next chapter, we look at depreciation and cash flow, two very important accounting concepts.

---

5. Stock that is repurchased by a firm is called Treasury stock. It is listed as a deduction from shareholders' equity in the amount paid to repurchase the stock, not its par value or the value for which it was originally sold.

Most students (and more than a few business executives) have trouble understanding the important accounting concepts of *depreciation* and *cash flow*. This usually happens because they do not understand the purpose of calculating depreciation, which (as we will soon see) is an important component of cash flow. Before the income tax was passed in 1913, equipment depreciated just as surely as it does today. However, accounting for depreciation was not given as much attention by management prior to 1913 as after because there were no tax aspects to consider.

The original idea, even before the income tax was passed, was that a firm should recognize that its plant and equipment was subject to wear and tear, and that the resulting reduction in value should be systematically taken into account on the firm's balance sheet. Years ago it was common practice for firms to list assets at cost on the asset side as long as they were in use. An account entitled Reserve for Depreciation (to reflect the accumulated depreciation to that point) was then maintained on the liabilities side just before the statement of shareholders' equity. Today virtually all firms show accumulated depreciation as an offset to each depreciable fixed asset or to depreciable fixed assets as a whole, as shown in Exhibit 2.1.[1]

	January 31,	
	1995	1994
Property, Plant and Equipment, at Cost:		
Land	3,036	2,741
Buildings and improvements	8,973	6,818
Fixtures and equipment	4,768	3,981
Transportation equipment	313	260
	17,090	13,800
Less accumulated depreciation	2,782	2,173
Net property, plant and equipment	14,308	11,627

Exhibit 2.1. Example of a modern way to account for depreciation. Adapted from 1995 Wal-Mart Stores *Annual Report*.

The purpose of computing depreciation is to allocate a portion of the costs of long term or fixed assets, particularly plant and equipment, as an expense in the years in which they are incurred.[2]

---

1. Only assets with an economic life of more than a year are placed on the balance sheet as an asset and depreciated. Assets with initial life of less than a year such as office supplies are expensed (charged as an expense) fully in the year in which they are acquired. Assets will small value and economic life greater than a year such as a pencil sharpener may also he expensed fully when purchased to simplify bookkeeping.

Some managers think of depreciation as a way to accumulate funds to replace an existing asset when it wears out. But this is not correct. Depreciation should be thought of as a way to recover the cost of an asset over its useful life. Most fixed assets must be acquired as a complete unit for a lump sum payment even though they provide services for several years.

Thus the cash outlay that eventually gives rise to the depreciation expense occurs at the time of acquisition, but the cost is charged against operations in future years using an acceptable method of calculating depreciation. Hence plant and equipment items represent a form of deferred costs that are "recouped" from sales revenues over the accounting life of the assets.[3]

There are two reasons why funds are not set aside each year and accumulated in a special account so money will be available to replace an asset (e.g., truck, machine tool) with one just like it when it wears out:

1. Management usually has better uses for its cash on a day to day basis than to keep it sitting in an account drawing a minimal rate of interest.
2. Improvements are constantly being made in most products. Thus if a machine (e.g., a personal computer or a truck) is replaced at some future date, it is very unlikely that it will be replaced with one exactly like it or at the same cost.

Nevertheless accumulating depreciation in a separate account (rather than writing down the value of the assets each year by the amount of depreciation charged) does serve to remind managers (and investors) that funds will be needed sometime in the future to purchase new plant and equipment, even if it is not possible to specify exactly what that plant and equipment will be or how much they will cost.

When a tax is imposed on the income that the firm earns, depreciation increases greatly in importance. Machines wear out just as before. But including the annual depreciation charges as an expense reduces the tax the company must pay. This is desirable, since the less money paid in income taxes (or the longer these payments can be deferred), the better. In fact, this leads to a working definition of depreciation that every manager should know (memorize):

Depreciation is a non-cash charge against earnings

It is a *non-cash* charge in the sense that depreciation does not result in an actual expenditure of cash. The amount of cash generated in a period is actually increased by the favorable effect deprecia-

---

2. If too little depreciation is charged to cover the cost of wear and tear on a machine, then when the machine has to be replaced a loss will be shown on the income statement equal to the amount of depreciation which had not been charged, but should have. Such entries violate the principle of matching revenues and expenses in the periods in which they occur and present a distorted view of the company's financial condition until corrected.

3. Depreciation in the accounting sense and the actual physical deterioration of assets may not coincide since it is difficult to accurately estimate the actual life of an asset when it is acquired. The accountant's primary concern is with apportioning the cost of an asset as a deduction from revenues over its useful life rather than in establishing its current market value, which may go up or down considerably over time.

tion charges have in reducing taxes paid in that period. The importance of depreciation in this regard can be seen from the pair of examples in Exhibit 2.2. The only difference is that depreciation is charged in one case and not in the other. The tax rate is assumed to be 50% in each case for ease of calculation.

Note the following effects:

1. When no depreciation is charged, net income is $20 and addition to cash is $20.
2. When depreciation is charged, net income is reduced by $10 but cash on hand in increased by $10 to $30.

The first result is simple enough, but the second requires some thought. Why is net income less but cash on hand more when depreciation is charged? The answer has to do with the concept of cash flow, defined as follows:

Cash flow = Net income + Depreciation

(Every manager should also memorize this definition).

XYZ Company Income Statement, 19XX				
No Depreciation Charged			**Depreciation Charged**	
Revenue	$100		Revenue	$100
CGS & SGA	60		CGS & SGA	60
—	—		Depreciation	20
Operating income	40		Operating income	20
Taxes (50%)	20		Taxes (50%)	10
Net income	$ 20		Net income	$ 10
Net income	$ 20		Net income	$ 10
+ Depreciation	—		+ Depreciation	20
= Cash flow	$ 20		= Cash flow	$ 30

Exhibit 2.2. Effect on cash flow of charging depreciation against revenues.

Since depreciation is charged against earnings, it has the effect of reducing net income. (This is the result of matching expenses, including depreciation, for each period with the corresponding revenues.) However, total cash on hand is increased because depreciation not only reduces net income but also reduces the amount of taxes to be paid. The reduction in taxes is exactly equal to the amount of depreciation charged times the tax rate. (In the example in Exhibit 2.2, $20 × .50 = $10.) The higher the tax rate, the more important depreciation becomes. Should the tax rate be zero (as in the case of a nonprofit organization), then depreciation would have no effect on cash flow or cash on hand. If the tax rate were 100%, then each dollar of depreciation would increase cash flow by one dollar.

In terms of planning a business, it is often more important to keep track of cash flow each year than net income. If depreciation charges are high in the first few years of a business, then *actual cash flow can be positive even if net income is negative*, as shown in Exhibit 2.3. Thus if a firm reports a loss (i.e., a negative net income) for a year, it may still be able to pay its bills for that year *if its cash flow is positive*.[4]

XYZ Company
Income Statement, 19XX

Revenue	$100
less: GCG & CGS	80
Depreciation	40 ←
Operating income	(20)
Taxes (assume 50%)	0
Net income	$(20) ←
Net income	$(20) ←
+ Depreciation	40 ←
= Cash flow	$20

Exhibit 2.3. Positive cash flow with negative net income.

Note that this would all be different if depreciation were not considered an expense for purposes of calculating taxes. If for some reason depreciation was defined to be similar to dividends and taken out of earnings *after* taxes, then it would not be of particular interest to the manager, except to alert him or her (as in the old days) that eventually the machinery will have to be replaced due to wear and tear.

Accountants have developed several methods of calculating depreciation for long term assets (those with an economic life of one year or more). The Internal Revenue Service specifies which method is acceptable for various classes of assets. The easiest and most logical way of computing depreciation is on a straight line basis. The underlying assumption is that a machine wears out at a uniform rate throughout its life. When planning new projects involving depreciable assets, general managers are encouraged to make the initial set of calculations using straight line depreciation. There are two reasons for doing so.

1. It is easier to compute. Remember, we are managers, not accountants.
2. It is conservative. Accelerating depreciation of an asset (e.g., a machine) can have some very desirable effects. It will improve cash flow in the early years of the asset's life when it may be

---

4. The term cash flow is occasionally used in reference to the actual flow of cash (e.g., dollars) in and out of a business on a periodic basis (e.g., monthly). This is important to monitor, but it is done independent of the accounting procedures used to prepare the balance sheet and income statement. This "cash flow" summary is analogous to maintaining a personal checking account (single entry bookkeeping). It is important not to overdraw, but the balance in the checking account is a poor measure of how well (or poorly) a person is doing. When finance and accounting executives talk about cash flow, they mean net income plus depreciation.

needed most. But keep in mind that if the results of a project are acceptable under straightline depreciation, they can only become more so using an accelerated method of depreciation. Hence it is conservative to evaluate the feasibility of projects using straight line depreciation.

ACCELERATED DEPRECIATION AND DEFERRED TAXES

The effects of accelerating depreciation are worth considering in more detail. Assume the XYZ Company purchases equipment at a cost of $100,000 that has a useful life of four years. Assume further that the company's sales are $100,000 and cost of goods sold is $60,000 for each of the next four years. The way depreciation is charged can have a significant effect on the timing of cash flow to the company, as demonstrated in Exhibit 2.4.

Firms commonly use different methods of depreciation for reporting to shareholders (financial reporting) and for computing taxes (tax reporting) for the IRS. When preparing annual reports for shareholders, as required by the Securities & Exchange Commission, firms almost always use straightline depreciation, since this results in higher net income and earnings per share than does the use of accelerated depreciation. However, firms often use accelerated depreciation for purposes of computing taxes. While accelerated depreciation lowers net income and earnings per share, it also generates higher cash flow, a feature considered desirable by managers.

Managers should be aware that the IRS requires corporate income tax returns to be prepared almost on a cash basis, meaning that taxes are due when payment is received. Financial reports (such as the annual report) are prepared using Generally Accepted Accounting Principles (GAAP), which are based on the principle of matching revenues and expenses to the period in which they occur. For example, a prepayment is counted for tax purposes when it is received, but is not counted for revenue until the service is provided, which could be in a later accounting period. The emphasis in this book is on meeting the requirements of GAAP.

Using accelerated depreciation for purposes of computing taxes and straight line depreciation for reporting to shareholders in the annual report gives rise to an entry on the balance sheet immediately before shareholders' equity called *deferred taxes*. Each year the difference between the taxes due using straight line depreciation and accelerated depreciation is added to this account, as shown in Exhibit 2.5. The deferred taxes account represents the amount of cash not spent on taxes that will be due at a future date. This is very desirable from the point of view of the company, since it is in effect receiving an interest free loan from the government equal to the amount of its deferred taxes. If new assets are placed in use each year and depreciated using accelerated depreciation, then the deferred taxes account will increase yearly and can become quite substantial. In fact, the change in deferred taxes from the preceding year to the current year can be considered a component of cash flow. Where the change in deferred taxes is significant, the definition now becomes:

Cash flow = Net income + Depreciation + Change in deferred taxes

Cash flow = Net Income + Depreciation

Straight Line Depreciation

	Year				4 Year
	1	2	3	4	Total
Revenues	100	100	100	100	400
CGS	60	60	60	60	240
Depreciation	25	25	25	25	100
Operating Income	15	15	15	15	60
Taxes (50%)	7.5	7.5	7.5	7.5	30
Net Income	7.5	7.5	7.5	7.5	30
Cash flow	32.5	32.5	32.5	32.5	130

Accelerated Depreciation

	Year				4 Year
	1	2	3	4	Total
Revenues	100	100	100	100	400
CGS	60	60	60	60	240
Depreciation	40	30	20	10	100
Operating Income	0	10	20	30	60
Taxes (50%)	0	5	10	15	30
Net Income	0	5	10	15	30
Cash flow	40	35	30	25	130

Computed for demonstration purposes using the "sum of the years' digits" method.

(e.g., year 1 = $\dfrac{4}{4+3+2+1}$; year 2 = $\dfrac{3}{4+3+2+1}$; etc.)

Exhibit 2.4. Cash flow with straight line and accelerated depreciation (figures in $000s).

	Year				
	1	2	3	4	Total
Taxes due (straight line basis)	7.5	7.5	7.5	7.5	30
Taxes paid (accelerated basis)	0	5.0	10.0	15.0	30
Deferred taxes (cumulative)	7.5	10.0	7.5	0	

Exhibit 2.5. Deferred taxes resulting from example in Exhibit 2.4.

DEFERRED TAX ASSETS

In the previous section we saw how accelerating depreciation led to an entry between long term debt and shareholders' equity called deferred taxes. More correctly, this should be called a *deferred tax liability*, since it represents an obligation to be paid in the future. This account may include other items involving temporary timing differences where a liability is recorded in one reporting period and paid in another one. However, deferred taxes due to accelerated depreciation is usually by far the largest component of this account.

Starting in 1993, many balance sheets show an entry called deferred taxes listed as a *current asset*. To non-accountants, this is a puzzling entry. At first glance, this entry might seem to be a reversal of a portion of the deferred tax liability. This is not so. Deferred taxes listed as a current asset arise from the requirements of SFAS 109, adopted in February 1992, which deals with temporary timing differences between recognition of certain expenses or income and calculation of taxes.

Consider a firm that rents property and receives a prepayment of $5,000 in December, 1994, for rent for January, 1995. The $5,000 is included in 1994 revenues for purposes of computing taxes, but is not included in revenue until 1995 for purposes of financial reporting. Assuming a marginal tax rate of 30%, the rental firm would pay $1,500 (.30 × $5,000) in taxes in 1994 on revenue it didn't include on its income statement until 1995. This tax payment is accounted for as a deferred tax asset in the amount of $1,500 on the balance sheet. The 1995 taxes on the $5,000 of income for January's rent will be $1,500. Since this amount has already been paid in 1994, the tax "payment" for 1995 will be made by reducing the deferred tax asset account by $1,500 rather than making a cash payment of $1,500.

Deferred tax assets can also arise when expenses incurred in one period, such as warranty claims, won't be paid until future years. Assume a firm knows from past experience that its warranty claims arising in future years from a product made during a particular year will be about $100,000. If that $100,000 was deducted in the year in which the product was made, it would result in a reduction of taxes of $30,000, assuming a marginal tax rate of 30%. As the $100,000 in warranty claims is charged against income in future years, taxes will be reduced by a total of $30,000, assuming the marginal tax rate remains the same.

In general, a deferred tax asset can arise in one of two ways:

- Revenue is received in one acounting period for tax purposes but is included in sales for reporting purposes in the next accounting period (e.g., year-end prepayment of rent).
- A liability incurred in one accounting period is deferred until a cash payment on it occurs in a future accounting period (e.g., warranty claims).

Understandably, some readers may find the whole subject of deferred taxes confusing. At the very least, they should know the following:

From a cash management point of view, a deferred tax liability is a deferral of a current obligation to a future time and is hence desirable. On the other hand, a deferred tax asset represents a prepayment of a future obligation, and is hence undesirable. A deferred tax asset is most easily understood if it is considered a prepayment, regardless of how it arises.

In practice, keeping track of deferred tax assets is quite complex and is best left to the accountants. However, the general manager should know how this entry arises, why it is a curent asset, and how its value is determined.[5]

TAXES AND THE TAX REFORM ACT OF 1986

The Tax Reform Act (TRA) of 1986 made major changes in federal tax policies for both individuals and corporations. The highest individual rate (28%) was *less* than the highest corporate tax rate (34%). Historically the highest individual rates were always greater than the top corporate rates. Here we will look at the federal income taxes as they apply to businesses. The TRA of 1986 replaced the system of computing depreciation known as the Accelerated Cost Recover System (ACRS) which was part of the Economic Recovery Tax Act (ERTA) of 1981. The TRA of 1986 uses a Modified Accelerated Cost Recovery System (MACRS) which is based on the declining balance method of depreciation.

The Economic Recovery Tax Act of 1981 had established an investment tax credit and an Accelerated Cost Recovery System (ACRS). The Tax Reform Act of 1986 repealed the investment tax credit for all equipment placed in service after January 1, 1986.[6] It also modified the ACRS system, which is now known as the Modified Accelerated Cost Recovery System (MACRS). An important modification was the extension of economic life for some classes of property (e.g., autos became five year rather than three year property). This had the effect of lengthening the asset's life, which in turn reduced the amount of depreciation charged on average per year.

The corporate tax rates for 1994 are shown in Exhibit 2.6.

If taxable income is over - -	But not over - -	Tax is:	Of the amount over - -
$0	$50,000	15%	$0
50,000	75,000	$7,500 + 25%	50,000
75,000	100,000	13,750 + 34%	75,000
100,000	335,000	22,250 + 39%	100,000
335,000	10,000,000	113,900 + 34%	335,000
10,000,000	15,000,000	3,400,000 + 35%	10,000,000
15,000,000	18,333,333	5,150,000 + 38%	15,000,000
18,333,333	- - -	35%	0

Exhibit 2.6. Tax rate schedule for corporations, 1994.

---

5. For a further discussion of deferred tax assets, see the current edition of *GAAP: Interpretation and Application of Generally Accepted Accounting Principles* (New York: John Wiley & Sons), Chapter 14, Accounting for Income Taxes.

6. The tax credit was calculated as a percent of the value of new plant and equipment placed in service during the tax year. It was then applied against taxes owed. Tax credits did not reduce the amount of depreciation that could be charged. They were designed as an incentive (and a very attractive one) for industry to modernize its plant and equipment.

CALCULATING DEPRECIATION UNDER MACRS

MACRS permits a choice of using accelerated or straight line depreciation systems. The main system uses accelerated depreciation and is referred to as the General Depreciation System (GDS). The other system uses straightline depreciation and is referred to as the Alternative Depreciation System (ADS). The procedure is similar in both cases and greatly facilitated by the extensive tables the Internal Revenue Service provides in its Publication 534 *Depreciation*, published annually.

The accelerated basis is described first because it is the method most businesses will use if they have a choice. For demonstration purposes assume a business has just purchased a new computer for $10,000. First find the computer's Recovery Period in years under the GDS (MACRS) heading in the Table of Class Lives and Recovery Periods in IRS Publication 534 *Depreciation*. The first page from this table is reproduced in Exhibit 2.7. Computers (under 00.12, Information Systems) have a MACRS Recovery Period of five years.

Now look in Exhibit 2.8 under the Recovery Period of five years to find the depreciation percentages to apply to the computer each year. The computer would be depreciated as follows:

Year 1: 20.00% of initial value, or	$ 2,000
Year 2: 32.00% of initial value, or	$ 3,200
Year 3: 19.20% of initial value, or	$ 1,920
Year 4: 11.52% of initial value, or	$ 1,152
Year 5: 11.52% of initial value, or	$ 1,152
Year 6: 5.76% of initial value, or	$ 576
Totals: 100%	$10,000

That is all there is to it. The percentages apply regardless of the value of the asset.

ALTERNATE (STRAIGHT LINE) DEPRECIATION SYSTEM

Businesses may elect to use the Alternate Depreciation System, which is a straight line method of depreciation with a half-year convention in place of the declining balance method. The calculation procedure is the same as before, except that now the ADS (right hand) column in the Table of Class Lives and Recovery Periods is used to find the Recovery Period. The appropriate table in IRS Publication 534 *Depreciation* is used to find the percentages to apply. Exhibit 2.9 gives selected values for the straight line depreciation option under MACRS when the half-year convention (explained later) is used. The computer has an Alternate MACRS Recovery Period of five years, same as under MACRS. It would now be depreciated as follows using the percentages from the third column of Exhibit 2.9.

Year 1: 10.00% of initial value, or	$ 1,000
Year 2: 20.00% of initial value, or	$ 2,000
Year 3: 20.00% of initial value, or	$ 2,000
Year 4: 20.00% of initial value, or	$ 2,000
Year 5: 20.00% of initial value, or	$ 2,000
Year 6: 10.00% of initial value, or	$ 1,000
Totals: 100%	$ 10,000

Table B-1. Table of Class Lives and Recovery Periods

Asset class	Description of assets included	Class Life (in years)	GDS (MACRS)	ADS
		Recovery Periods (in years)		
SPECIFIC DEPRECIABLE ASSETS USED IN ALL BUSINESS ACTIVITIES, EXCEPT AS NOTED:				
00.11	**Office Furniture, Fixtures, and Equipment:** Includes furniture and fixtures that are not a structural component of a building. Includes such assets as desks, files, safes, and communications equipment. Does not include communications equipment that is included in other classes.	10	7	10
00.12	**Information Systems:** Includes computers and their peripheral equipment used in administering normal business transactions and the maintenance of business records, their retrieval and analysis. Information systems are defined as: 1) Computers: A computer is a programmable electronically activated device capable of accepting information, applying prescribed processes to the information, and supplying the results of these processes with or without human intervention. It usually consists of a central processing unit containing extensive storage, logic, arithmetic, and control capabilities. Excluded from this category are adding machines, electronic desk calculators, etc., and other equipment described in class 00.13. 2) Peripheral equipment consists of the auxiliary machines which are designed to be placed under control of the central processing unit. Nonlimiting examples are: Card readers, card punches, magnetic tape feeds, high speed printers, optical character readers, tape cassettes, mass storage units, paper tape equipment, keypunches, data entry devices, teleprinters, terminals, tape drives, disc drives, disc files, disc packs, visual image projector tubes, card sorters, plotters, and collators. Peripheral equipment may be used on-line or off-line. Does not include equipment that is an integral part of other capital equipment that is included in other classes of economic activity, i.e., computers used primarily for process or production control, switching, channeling, and automating distributive trades and services such as point of sale (POS) computer systems. Also, does not include equipment of a kind used primarily for amusement or entertainment of the user.	6	5	5
00.13	**Data Handling Equipment; except Computers:** Includes only typewriters, calculators, adding and accounting machines, copiers, and duplicating equipment.	6	5	6
00.21	**Airplanes (airframes and engines), except those used in commercial or contract carrying of passengers or freight, and all helicopters (airframes and engines)**	6	5	6
00.22	**Automobiles, Taxis**	3	5	5
00.23	**Buses**	9	5	9
00.241	**Light General Purpose Trucks:** Includes trucks for use on the road (actual weight less than 13,000 pounds).	4	5	5
00.242	**Heavy General Purpose Trucks:** Includes heavy general purpose trucks, concrete ready mix-trucks, and ore trucks, for use over the road (actual unloaded weight 13,000 pounds or more).	6	5	6
00.25	**Railroad Cars and Locomotives, except those owned by railroad transportation companies**	15	7	15
00.26	**Tractor Units for Use Over-The-Road**	4	3	4
00.27	**Trailers and Trailer-Mounted Containers**	6	5	6
00.28	**Vessels, Barges, Tugs, and Similar Water Transportation Equipment, except those used in marine construction**	18	10	18
00.3	**Land Improvements:** Includes improvements directly to or added to land, whether such improvements are section 1245 property or section 1250 property, provided such improvements are depreciable. Examples of such assets might include sidewalks, roads, canals, waterways, drainage facilities, sewers (not including municipal sewers in Class 51), wharves and docks, bridges, fences, landscaping shrubbery, or radio and television transmitting towers. Does not include land improvements that are explicitly included in any other class, and buildings and structural components as defined in section 1.48–1(e) of the regulations. Excludes public utility initial clearing and grading land improvements as specified in Rev. Rul. 72-403, 1972-2 C.B. 102.	20	15	20
00.4	**Industrial Steam and Electric Generation and/or Distribution Systems:** Includes assets, whether such assets are section 1245 property or 1250 property, providing such assets are depreciable, used in the production and/or distribution of electricity with rated total capacity in excess of 500 Kilowatts and/or assets used in the production and/or distribution of steam with rated total capacity in excess of 12,500 pounds per hour for use by the taxpayer in its industrial manufacturing process or plant activity and not ordinarily available for sale to others. Does not include buildings and structural components as defined in section 1.48–1(e) of the regulations. Assets used to generate and/or distribute electricity or steam of the type described above, but of lesser rated capacity, are not included, but are included in the appropriate manufacturing equipment classes elsewhere specified. Also includes electric generating and steam distribution assets, which may utilize steam produced by a waste reduction and resource recovery plant, used by the taxpayer in its industrial manufacturing process or plant activity. Steam and chemical recovery boiler systems used for the recovery and regeneration of chemicals used in manufacturing, with rated capacity in excess of that described above, with specifically related distribution and return systems are not included but are included in appropriate manufacturing equipment classes elsewhere specified. An example of an excluded steam and chemical recovery boiler system is that used in the pulp and paper manufacturing equipment classes elsewhere specified. An example of an excluded steam and chemical recovery boiler system is that used in the pulp and paper manufacturing industry.	22	15	22

Exhibit 2.7.   Table of Class Lives and Recovery Periods. Source: IRS Publication 534 *Depreciation* for use in preparing 1994 returns, p. 71.

Recovery Period in years						
Recovery Year:	3 years	5 years	7 years	10 years	15 years	20 years
1	33.33	20.00	14.29	10.00	5.00	3.750
2	44.45	32.00	24.49	18.00	9.50	7.219
3	14.81*	19.20	17.49	14.40	8.55	6.677
4	7.41	11.52*	12.49	11.52	7.70	6.177
5		11.52	8.93*	9.22	6.93	5.713
6		5.76	8.92	7.37	6.23	5.285
7			8.93	6.55*	5.90*	4.888
8			4.46	6.55	5.90	4.522
9				6.56	5.91	4.462*
10				6.55	5.90	4.461
11				3.28	5.91	4.462
12					5.90	4.461
13					5.91	4.462
14					5.90	4.461
15					5.91	4.462
16					2.95	4.461
17						4.462
18						4.461
19						4.462
20						4.461
21						2.231

* Year of switch to straight line to maximize depreciation deduction.
Note: 3, 5, 7 and 10 year Recovery Periods are calculated using 200% declining balance; 15 and 20 year Recovery Periods are calculated using 150% declining balance.

Exhibit 2.8. Asset depreciation percentages under MACRS (percent of depreciable basis) for half-year convention. Adapted from Table A-1 of IRS Publication 534 *Depreciation* for use in preparing 1994 Returns.

Businesses should prefer to use the standard or GDS MACRS depreciation system because it accelerates depreciation charges and hence reduces taxes and increases cash flow in the early years of an asset's life.[7]

Remember there are situations where special rules may apply, especially when several assets are involved. Thus when calculating depreciation for tax purposes, always consult the latest edition of IRS Publication 534 *Depreciation* to be sure the rules that are currently applicable are followed.

---

7. Businesses must use the Alternate Depreciation System in a few situations, such as when the property is predominantly used outside the United States or the property ts tax exempt. In general, businesses doing business inside the United States can elect to use the GDS (accelerated) MARS depreciation percentages rather than the ADS (straight line) depreciation percentages.

				Recovery Period in years					
Recovery Year:	3	4	5	6	7	8	9	10
1	16.67	12.50	10.00	8.33	7.14	6.25	5.56	5.00
2	33.33	25.00	20.00	16.67	14.29	12.50	11.11	10.00
3	33.33	25.00	20.00	16.67	14.29	12.50	11.11	10.00
4	16.67	25.00	20.00	16.67	14.28	12.50	11.11	10.00
5		12.50	20.00	16.66	14.29	12.50	11.11	10.00
6			10.00	16.67	14.28	12.50	11.11	10.00
7				8.33	14.29	12.50	11.11	10.00
8					7.14	12.50	11.11	10.00
9						6.25	11.11	10.00
10							5.56	10.00
11								5.00

Exhibit 2.9. Selected MACRS depreciation percentages for the straight line method (assuming half-year convention).

SOME QUESTIONS AND ANSWERS ON MACRS

Q: If an asset's life is five years, then why is it depreciated over six years as in the example of the computer just given?

A: The TRA of 1986 includes a half-year convention which means that all property is treated as if it were placed in service and disposed of at mid-year, regardless of when it was actually placed in use or disposed of. The first year an asset is placed in use only half the full amount of depreciation computed is counted. The last year is also a half year by convention. Thus deductions for depreciation are spread over one more year than the Recovery Period of the asset. This was done deliberately to reduce slightly the extent to which depreciation had previously been accelerated under ACRS.

By reducing the degree to which depreciation is accelerated, the government raises more money sooner from the income tax because deductions are less in the early years of an asset's life. This is one way the government hoped to raise revenue to offset the reductions in the personal and corporate tax rates in the TRA of 1986. Two other major ways were the elimination of the investment tax credit and the elimination of preferential tax treatment for capital gains.

Q: Do I need to actually compute depreciation using the declining balance method for every asset I have?

A: No. You don't need to know how to perform the declining balance depreciation calculations at all. What you do need to know is how to find the correct depreciation percentages from the tables in IRS Publication 534 *Depreciation* to apply to each of your assets.

Q: Suppose I want to know how to actually calculate depreciation using the double declining balance method?

A: Look in an accounting textbook that was published prior to 1981 or after 1986 for an explanation. The declining balance method of depreciation was one of several methods allowed by the IRS until the Economic Recovery Tax Act of 1981 implemented the ACRS system, which no longer permitted use of the declining balance method.

SECTION 179 DEDUCTION

A Section 179 deduction is an important provision in the tax code. Currently up to $17,500 of equipment can be expensed in the year in which it is purchased. However, the $17,500 is reduced dollar for dollar where the cost of the equipment placed in service during a tax year exceeds $200,000. When total investment in qualified property exceeds $217,500, the election to expense $17,500 of equipment no longer applies. For small businesses, the $17,500 provision can be very helpful, especially for assets that quickly lose their value such as personal computers. This points out that the ultimate in accelerated depreciation is to expense an asset fully in the year in which it is acquired. Note that if the new computer just used as an example was counted as a Section 179 deduction, it would never show up as an asset on the balance sheet even though it cost $10,000 and had a Recovery Period (economic life) of five years!

AN EXCEPTION: THE UNITS OF PRODUCTION METHOD

Property that can be depreciated on a basis other than a term of years may be excluded from MACRS. For example, the *units of production* method may be used to depreciate a machine rather than MACRS. Here the machine's cost is divided by the estimated number of units to be produced to get depreciation per unit produced. Depreciation for the year is then the depreciation per unit times the units produced during the year. If appropriate, machine hours could be used rather than units produced.

FREE CASH FLOW ANALYSIS

In the 1980s, the term "free cash flow" came into common usage, especially among Wall Street analysts and takeover artists. The idea is to find out how much cash a firm generates, because cash can be used to pay the interest charges incurred when a large amount of debt is used to acquire a firm. It can also be used to estimate if a firm will need to borrow money in the future. Free cash flow is defined as follows:

Free cash flow = Cash flow − Capital expenditures − Dividends

The *Value Line Investment Survey* provides an easy way to estimate free cash flow for the 1,700 stocks it covers. The sheet for each company gives cash flow per share, dividends per share, capital spending per share and shares outstanding. Free cash flow per share is found by subtracting capital expenditures per share and dividends per share from cash flow per share. Free cash flow is then equal to free cash flow per share times shares outstanding. If free cash flow is a negative number, it is quite likely the firm will have to increase its long term debt. If free cash flow is large, as is typically the case with food companies, then the firm may become a target for a takeover artist. General Foods, Kraft and Nabisco are examples of food companies with large free cash flows that were acquired In the 1980s.

EXAMPLES OF FREE CASH FLOW ANALYSIS

Exhibit 2.11 shows a free cash flow analysis for one of America's most profitable firms, the Kellogg Company of Battle Creek, Michigan. Kellogg is the world's largest manufacturer of ready-to-eat cereals, with 37% of the U.S. market and 50% of the world-wide market. Data on cash flow per share, dividends per share, and capital spending per share are taken from the Value Line sheet for Kellogg shown in Exhibit 2.12.

The analysis in Exhibit 2.11 shows that Kellogg is a very profitable company. It has increased its dividend and funded about $400,000,000 of capital spending each year. It still has generated "excess cash" of about one billion dollars for this four-year period. Exhibit 2.11 also shows that Kellogg has used some of this money to repurchase shares, as shares outstanding have fallen from 237 million in 1992 to 216 million in 1995.

	1992	1993	1994	1995E
Cash flow/share	3.74	4.15	4.34	4.70
- dividends/share	1.20	1.32	1.40	1.48
- capital spending/share	2.00	1.97	1.60	1.60
Free cash flow/share	0.54	0.86	1.34	1.62
x Shares outstanding (000,000s)	237	228	222	216
= Free cash flow ($000,000s)	128.7	196.1	398.6	349.9
Total free cash flow, 1992 - 1995	$1,073,300,000			

Exhibit 2.11. Free Cash Flow Analysis, Kellogg Company. Source of data: *Value Line Investment Survey*, May 19, 1995, p. 1483.

Exhibit 2.13 shows a free cash flow analysis for the same years for Weyerhaeuser, the world's largest private owner of softwood timber. Weyerhaeuser is in a highly capital intensive business. Data on cash flow per share, dividends per share, and capital spending per share are taken from the Value Line sheet for Weyerhaeuser shown in Exhibit 2.14.

The free cash flow analysis for Weyerhaeuser shows quite a different picture than it did for Kellogg. It has an accumulated negative cash flow of nearly $500,000,000 for 1992-1995. Because of this, dividend increases, if any, are likely to be small and infrequent. A blank Free Cash Flow Analysis sheet is included in Appendix A. The sheet is arranged so that entries are on a per share basis to permit direct use of company data from the *Value Line Investment Survey*, which covers approximately 1,800 publicly held companies. Value Line also excludes any non-cash charges, such as for restructuring, from its figures. The information needed to perform a free cash flow analysis should also be available from a firm's annual report, although it probably won't be arranged so conveniently.

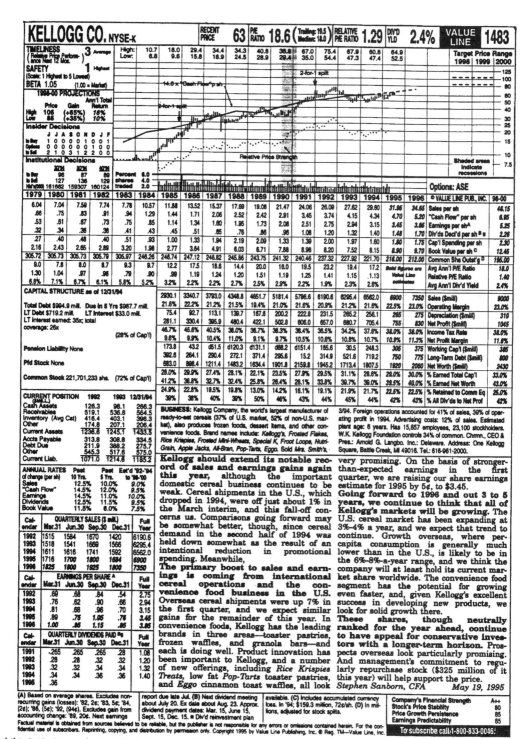

	1992	1993	1994	1995E
Cash flow/share	4.28	4.63	5.46	7.55
- dividends/share	1.20	1.20	1.20	1.20
- capital spending/share	3.02	4.72	5.36	6.05
Free cash flow/share	0.06	(1.29)	(1.10)	–0–
x Shares outstanding (000,000s)	204	205	206	206
= Free cash flow ($000,000s)	12.2	(264.5)	(226.6)	–0–
Total free cash flow, 1992 - 1995		$ (478,900,000)		

Exhibit 2.13. Free Cash Flow Analysis, Weyerhaeuser Company. Source of data: *Value Line Investment Survey*, July 21, 1995, p. 941.

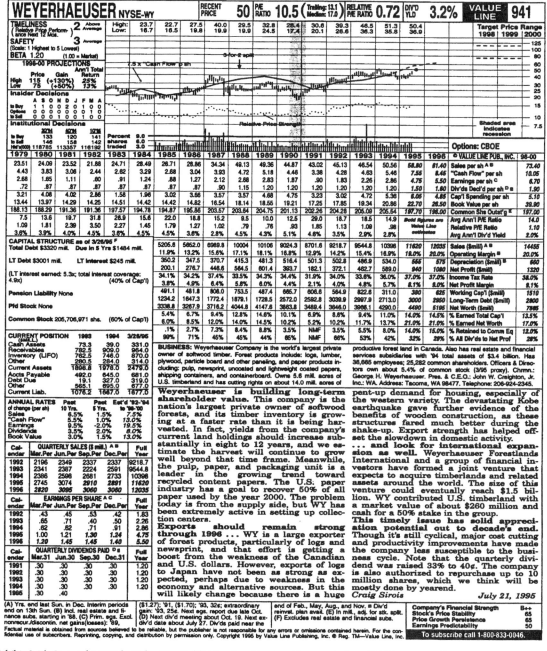

Exhibit 2.14. Copyright 1995 by Value Line Publishing, Inc. Reprinted by permission; All Rights reserved.

SUMMARY

This chapter has illustrated the importance of depreciation and its effect on cash flow from the point of view of the general manager. It has also provided a brief introduction to the MACRS system which offers a choice of accelerated or straight line depreciation. Remember, straight line depreciation is always an acceptable way to depreciate an asset, even though there are usually tax advantages associated with accelerating depreciation.

Current editions of Internal Revenue Service publications should be reviewed carefully before actually computing depreciation under MACRS. IRS Publication 534 *Depreciation* discusses depreciation methods in detail. IRS Publication 334 *Tax Guide for Small Business* may also be helpful in determining how to calculate depreciation for small businesses. Proper implementation requires paying close attention to the many definitions and exceptions inherent in MACRS, and is a task best left to the firm's accountants.

While the general manager doesn't need to know how to prepare the income statement and the balance sheet (finance and accounting experts can be relied on to do that), he or she should know how to evaluate a firm's financial condition using *ratio analysis*. This can be done in straightforward fashion by calculating a set of nine common ratios which, taken together, will yield insights into the financial condition of the firm which may not otherwise be apparent.

Pocket calculators have greatly facilitated the arithmetic associated with ratio analysis. However, use common sense when doing the calculations since ratios are rarely accurate to more than two significant figures.[1] For example, 12,674,761/7,417,614 = 1.7087382 (a ridiculous number of decimal places!) can be approximated by 12,674/7,417 = 1.71 (perfectly satisfactory) or even 12.6/7.4 = 1.7 (usually satisfactory). In general, ratios should be carried out to one decimal place (e.g., 0.5, 1.5) or three significant figures (e.g., 123, 12.3 or 1.23).

NINE USEFUL RATIOS

The number of ratios that could be calculated is practically unlimited.[2] However, the nine basic ratios described below are usually sufficient to evaluate the financial health of a firm. Keep in mind that all the ratios are not equally relevant to a given situation, and no one ratio of itself will tell the whole story. Acceptable values of one or more ratios may vary considerably by industry or company situation. It's a good idea to calculate all nine ratios for more than one year to see if any trends are evident. Where appropriate, a typical value of the ratio is given after the title.

1. Current Ratio (1.5 : 1)

The current ratio is a basic test of the firm's ability to pay its bills.

$$\text{Current} = \frac{\text{Current assets}}{\text{Current liabilities}}$$

This ratio tells how many times the current assets can cover the current liabilities. While current

---

1. A ratio is a relationship between two numbers. If one of the numbers is unusually large or small (e.g., zero or near zero), ratios may give nonsensical results. Hence always use common sense when interpreting ratios. Pocket calculators greatly facilitate calculation of ratios. However, they typically provide much more precision than the data merits. *Precision* refers to the number of places or digits in the answer (e.g., 1.234567), while *accuracy* refers to the number of significant digits (e.g., 1.2). A word of caution on the use of calculators is also in order. Always ask yourself if the ratio (result) obtained is *reasonable*. If it isn't, redo the calculation to make sure you didn't make an error entering data or using the calculator.

2. See, for example, Sheldon Gates, *101 business Ratios* (Scottsdale, AZ: McLane Publications, 1993).

ratios range widely, a rule of thumb that cuts across most industries is 1.5 : 1.

Major components of current assets and current liabilities are as follows:

Current Assets	Current Liabilities
Cash	Accounts payable
Cash equivalents (government securities)	Payroll
Accounts receivable	Taxes due
Inventory	Current portion of long term debt
Deferred taxes	

Historically, the standard for the current ratio was 2 : 1. However, with better cash management techniques and a trend toward just-in-time inventory systems, the general standard for the current ratio is now closer to 1.5 : 1. For well run manufacturing firms, it may fall as low as 1 : 1. This means that working capital, which is defined as current assets minus current liabilities, will be zero when the current ratio is 1 : 1.

The current ratio can also be used to estimate a firm's *excess cash*, or money that is not needed for daily operation of the business. First, assume a desired current ratio, such as 2 : 1. Then find the firm's current liabilities. The current assets necessary to maintain a current ratio of 2 : 1 are then equal to two times the current liabilities. Anything more than this amount can be considered excess cash.

$$\text{Excess cash estimate} = \text{Current assets} - 2 \times \text{Current liabilities}$$

On December 31st, 1994 the Stryker Corporation had current assets of $540 million and current liabilities of $179 million. Its excess cash would thus be equal to

$$\$540,000,000 - 2 \times \$179,000,000 = \$182,000,000$$

If a current ratio of 1.5 : 1 were assumed, this procedure would lead to even more excess cash for the Stryker Corporation. The excess cash calculation should be done for several years. Rapidly growing companies, such as Stryker, may accumulate significant amounts of cash for a few years in anticipation of a major acquisition or capital spending program.

2. Liquidity Ratio or "Acid Test" (0.5 : 1)

The current ratio may be a meaningless number if some of the current assets are in fact not very liquid. Thus a company might have a current ratio of 2 : 1 but have eighty percent of its current assets in hard to sell inventory. In such a situation the company can only meet its current liabilities with, at best, twenty percent of its current assets.

The liquidity ratio, sometimes called the "acid test," tries to give a more realistic picture of the firm's liquidity. It is calculated by taking all accounts above inventory (cash and assets readily convertible to cash) and dividing them by the current liabilities.

$$\text{Liquidity ratio} = \frac{\text{Liquid current assets}}{\text{Current liabilities}}$$

The rule of thumb is 0.5 : 1. Keep in mind that on a properly prepared balance sheet the most liquid assets (e.g., cash) are listed first and the least liquid last. In firms where there is no inventory (e.g., natural gas exploration, consulting firms) the current ratio will be about the same as the liquidity ratio.

In large retailing firms, such as Wal-Mart, the liquidity ratio is often considerably below 0.5. Wal-Mart typically has only a few days of receivables and payable of 30 days or more. Cash that is not needed to pay bills is put into inventory, which runs over 70 days. Wal-Mart's outstanding financial performance shows that a liquidity ratio of 0.5 or less should be considered standard for large retailing firms.

Only assets listed above inventory on the balance sheet should be used when calculating the liquidity ratio. Any current assets listed below inventory are presumably less liquid than inventory and hence are excluded.

3. Receivables (30 Days)

The speed with which customers pay their bill is directly reflected in a firm's working capital needs.[3] Since most businesses expect their customers to pay within thirty days, the average accounts receivable outstanding should be about thirty days. Assuming each month has thirty days and a year has 360 days for ease of calculation, the following ratio gives an approximation of the average days receivables:

$$\text{Receivables (days)} = \frac{\text{Accounts receivable}}{\text{Annual sales}} \times 360$$

Annual sales are gross sales minus returns and discounts. This equation can be arrived by considering that receivables expressed in days are to 360 days in a year as receivables expressed in dollars are to annual sales expressed in dollars, or graphically as follows:

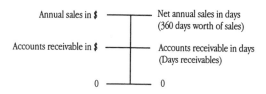

---

3. Working capital is defined as the difference between current assets (including inventory) and current liabilities. If working capital is negative, it means that current assets are less than current liabilities and some long term assets are being financed by current liabilities rather than by long term debt or shareholders' equity. For years, McDonald's, the leading fast food chain, has operated with negative working capital.

$$\frac{\text{Accounts receivable in days}}{360 \text{ days worth of sales}} = \frac{\text{Accounts receivables in \$}}{\text{Annual sales in \$}}$$

$$\text{or} \quad \text{Receivables (days)} = \frac{\text{Accounts receivable}}{\text{Annual sales}} \times 360$$

Most retailing firms have primarily cash (or credit card) sales, which is reflected in days receivables of only one or two days.

If a firm has its own credit card, then its receivables will be much higher than one or two days. For example, The Limited has credit cards for several of its divisions. In 1993, its receivables, including credit card sales of $1 billion, were 52.5 days. If credit card receivables of $978 million are removed, then the receivables would fall to 3.9 days. Since the annual interest charged on credit card accounts can be as high as 20 percent, it is very attractive for firms to have their own credit cards.

4. Payables (30 Days)

The calculation of days payables is similar to that of days receivables, except cost of goods sold is used in place of sales.

$$\text{Payables (days)} = \frac{\text{Accounts payable} \times 360}{\text{Cost of goods sold}}$$

As with days receivables, the standard is about thirty days. The purpose of this ratio is to see how rapidly a firm pays its bills, realizing that the longer the payables period, the more interest free loans the firm has and the more angry creditors as well![4]

It is important to watch the trend for receivables and payables. A lengthening of the payables period (e.g. from 30 to 45 days) together with a shortening of the accounts receivable period (e.g. from 30 to 15 days) is often a sign of an immediate cash problem and a low liquidity ratio. The firm is trying to get its money as soon as it can and delay paying its bill as long as possible.

Some companies pay their bills as soon as they are received, not realizing that supplier credit is an interest free loan. Once a company has established the habit of paying quickly it may be difficult to

---

4. Large retailing firms such as Wal-Mart and Sears often have figures for days payable of 45 days or more. Because it is do desirable to sell to a large chain, many suppliers will wait up to 45 days for payment in order to keep the account. This practice, together with a days receivables period of less than five days, can give retailers interest free use of a large amount of money.

Consider Wal-Mart, which in 1995 had payables of $5.9 billion and receivables of only $700 million. Wal-Mart had the use of the difference, over five *billion* dollars, on which it did not pay any interest. F or Wal-Mart and many other large retailers, this amounts to a quasi-permanent (and very attractive) form of financing.

An even better arrangement, from the firm's point of view, is the situation where there are sizable prepayments for services not yet rendered, such as season tickets, traveler's checks or insurance premiums. Prepayments are accounted for by adding them to cash on the asset side, then creating a liability in an equal amount called something like customer deposits or revenue billed and collected in advance. As the service is rendered, the liability is reduced and sales credited (increased) by the value of the service rendered.

take advantage of supplier credit because the change in payment patterns is immediately obvious to a firm's creditors and usually causes some concern. On the other hand, a company that is always fairly slow in making payments should cause little concern when it takes sixty days to pay a bill because that is its normal habit.

Some firms will make a point of paying bills within a much shorter period of time, often ten days, to take advantage of trade discounts offered by creditors. The terms 2/10, net/30 indicate that the buyer is offered a two percent discount if the bill is paid within ten days. If not paid within ten days, the full amount of the bill is due within thirty days, or finance charges may be added to it.

Trade credit can be a very expensive form of financing when a cash discount is offered. If the terms of sales are 2/10, net/30, the firm has the use of funds for an additional twenty days if it does not take the discount but pays on the final day of th net period. In the case of a $100 invoice, it would have the use of $98 (the amount it would have had to pay at the end of ten days) for twenty days. The annual interest cost is 36.7%! (It costs $2 to have the use of $98 for 20 days, or on an annual basis, $2/98 x 360 days/20 days = 36.7%) It is almost always wise to take advantage of such trade discounts. A financially healthy firm which shows payables of about ten days is probably doing just that.

5. Inventory (60-90 Days for Manufacturing Firms; 30 Days for Other Firms)

In many businesses the speed with which inventory is turned over or used up essentially determines the cash requirements because inventories are usually the largest user of cash in times of expansion.[5] The days of inventory on hand is calculated by:

$$\text{Inventory (days)} = \frac{\text{Inventory}}{\text{Cost of goods sold}} \times 360 \text{ days}$$

If the cost of goods sold figure is not given, it may be necessary to estimate cost of goods by assuming it is a certain percentage (e.g., 80%) of sales. Sometimes the relationship is expressed as inventory turnover so that:

$$\text{Inventory turnover/year} = \frac{\text{Cost of goods sold}}{\text{Inventory}}$$

How fast inventory should turn over rests entirely with the industry, company and previous history. Twelve times a year (once a month) is a commonly used rule of thumb. Generally the higher the inventory turnover figure, the more efficient the inventory management of the firm. However, a relatively high inventory turnover ratio may be the result of too low a level of inventory and frequent

---

5. Inventory in a manufacturing firm equals the sum of raw materials, work in process and finished goods. In a service firm it is inventory in stock. Some firms, such as electric utilities, may have no inventory or finished goods. Output is supplied to the user as soon as it is generated. Inventories in manufacturing firms tend to run higher than 30 days. Figures of 60-90 days are common in many well run manufacturing firms. But remember, it is very expensive to hold inventory. Holding costs such as insurance, utilities, taxes and security can easily amount to 25% or more of the value of the inventory over the course of a year.

stockouts. It might also be the result of too many small orders for inventory replenishment. Either situation may be more costly to the company than carrying a larger investment in inventory and having a lower turnover ratio.

Inventory turnover figures may be distorted if there has been a major write-down of inventories during one or more of the periods being analyzed. Firms dealing with commodities (e.g., silver, crude oil, timber) many occasionally experience considerable increases in the value of their inventories due to increases in the market price of the commodity.

It would be more accurate in calculating the inventory ratios to use an *average inventory* for the year, but unless there are severe fluctuations from year to year, the ending inventory (usually chosen to avoid cyclical peaks or valleys) is adequate. Firms that employ the Japanese *kan-ban* or just in time inventory system may show much lower inventory figures than is standard in their industry.

6. Debt to Equity (<.5)

For large firms (e.g., sales over $10,000,000) this ratio is defined as:

$$\text{Debt/Equity} = \frac{\text{Long term debt}}{\text{Shareholders' equity}}$$

The trend over time is most important, although as a conservative rule of thumb long term debt should not exceed one half of shareholders' equity (see page six). The greater the amount of long term debt, the greater the effects of financial leverage, favorable in good times and unfavorable in bad times.[6] Under cyclical conditions a firm with no long term debt (and no interest charges) will have a steadier earnings per share record than a firm with substantial long term debt (and high interest charges).

Should deferred taxes be included as part of long term debt? Even though the entry appears just before long term debt, the answer is no. The reason is that there is no interest associated with deferred taxes, while there is interest associated with long term debt. The deferred tax entry results from timing differences between when tax is due and when revenues and expenses are counted.

Using this reasoning, capital lease obligations should be included as part of long term debt. They represent an obligation of the firm and have an interest rate associated with them. In general, an entry after deferred taxes and before shareholders' equity should be included as part of long term debt only if it has an interest charge associated with it.

When goodwill and other intangible assets (ones listed below goodwill) are significant (more than ten percent of total assets), they should be deducted from net worth (as shareholders' equity is often called in this context) to obtain the *tangible* net worth of the firm. Tangible net worth is what

---

6. Leverage is discussed in Chapter 5.

the firm would theoretically be worth if it went out of business, or the excess of tangible assets over all liabilities.

Should preferred stock be included in shareholders' equity? There is no clear cut answer since preferred stock is midway between long term debt and equity. It represents a fixed prior claim on earnings, and thus from a shareholder's point of view it is usually viewed as a form of long term debt. Some managers like to view preferred stock as a form of equity because doing so will increase the firm's equity base, reduce its debt to equity ratio and, presumably, increase its capacity for long term debt.

Small firms may be unable to obtain long term financing and hence will often show a high amount of short term debt and no long term debt. Therefore total debt (which may be all short term debt) should be used when calculating the debt/equity ratio for a small firm.

$$\text{Debt/Equity for small firms} = \frac{\text{Total debt}}{\text{Shareholders' equity}}$$

However, short term debt usually has a higher interest rate and is more sensitive to interest rate changes because it is subject to frequent renewal. As a business grows, it is common for long term debt to be issued to replace short term debt.

7. Assets to Sales (1 : 1 Average)

The assets to sales ratio serves as a reminder of how much in assets is necessary to support an incremental dollar of sales.

$$\text{Assets to sales} = \frac{\text{Total tangible assets}}{\text{Sales}}$$

where

$$\text{Total tangible assets} = \begin{array}{l}\text{Total assets less Intangible} \\ \text{assets (e.g., goodwill and} \\ \text{items below goodwill on the} \\ \text{balance sheet)}\end{array}$$

The assets/sales ratio for a Fortune 500 firm is typically about 1 : 1. This relationship can be used to estimate a firm's assets only if its sales are known. The assets/sales ratios for ten Fortune 500 U.S. corporations in 1994 are given in Exhibit 3.1. A word of caution is in order in calculating assets/sales ratios. Since 1990, U.S. firms have included the assets and liabilities of finance subsidiaries on the balance sheet of the parent company. For firms with significant finance subsidiaries, such as Ford, General Electric and General Motors, the assets/sales calculation will seem unusually high for a predominantly manufacturing firm unless the finance subsidiary's assets are removed first.

Company	Sales[a]	Assets[a]	Assets/Sales
Exxon	101.5	87.8	.87
IBM	64.0	81.1	1.27
Procter & Gamble	30.3	25.5	.84
Dayton Hudson	21.3	11.7	.55
Eastman Kodak	16.9	15.0	.89
Coca-Cola	16.2	13.9	.86
Caterpillar	14.3	16.3	1.14
Delta Airlines	12.4	11.9	.96
Anheuser-Busch	12.1	11.0	.91
Compaq Computer	10.9	6.2	.57

[a]Figures in $ billions.

Exhibit 3.1. Assets to sales ratios for ten Fortune 500 firms, 1994.

Use caution when interpreting the assets/sales ratio. A low value, which is usually desirable, can arise two ways, only one of which is good.

A. High labor productivity (the good way). This serves to increase the sales produced per dollar value of asset and hence reduce the assets/sales ratio. A tipoff to high labor productivity is a sales per employee figure which is much higher than the industry average. In 1994 sales per employee for a Fortune 500 industrial firm was about $200,000. However, labor intensive service businesses such as fast foods will be considerably less; in 1994 sales per employee at McDonald's averaged $45,000. Asset intensive businesses such as oil refining will be considerably higher; in 1994 sales per employee at Exxon averaged $1.2 million.

B. Heavily depreciated equipment (the bad way). This serves to reduce the numerator in the assets to sales ratio, and hence reduce the value of the ratio itself. A firm with heavily depreciated equipment may not be able to sustain its current level of sales for long. If accumulated depreciation is more than half of the original value of the assets, this is a good indication that assets are old and will soon need replacing.[7]

---

7. Remember that the depreciation figures given in an annual report are almost always calculated using the straight line method as allowed by the Securities and Exchange Commission. Accelerated depreciation, which may more accurately reflect the condition of the assets, may have been used for tax purposes. Hence the annual report is more likely to understate rather than overstate the actual condition of plant and equipment.

8. Return on Sales (5%, With Wide Variation by Industry)

Return on sales refers to how much the company earns after tax on each dollar of sales.

$$\text{Return on sales} = \frac{\text{Net income}}{\text{Sales}}$$

In general, the higher the return on sales the better, although a good figure varies widely by industry. Most manufacturing firms have a return on sales of about five percent. Food stores may have a return on sales of only a percent or so, but make their money on high volume. Pharmaceutical firms such as Lilly, Merck and Upjohn typically have a return on sales of ten percent or more.

9. Return on Equity (Minimum of 15%)

Return on equity (ROE) is an extremely important ratio which indicates what rate of return the common stockholders are getting on their investment. It is calculated as follows:

$$\text{Return on equity} = \frac{\text{Net income}}{\text{Shareholders' equity}}$$

where

Net income = Income after taxes and before dividends

Values for ROE vary by industry and by capital structure.[8] However, ROE for a typical ongoing business should be consistently above the amount an investor could get on a perfectly secure alternative investment (e.g., government securities such as ninety day Treasury bills). Most well run firms will consistently return fifteen percent or more on their equity. An ROE significantly above fifteen percent may indicate a new firm with a very successful product, a risky business with a commensurately higher return, a firm with very low shareholders' equity reflecting losses from one or more preceding years, or a highly leveraged firm.

USING RATIOS TO EVALUATE A FIRM'S FINANCIAL HEALTH

The purpose of ratio analysis is to get a feeling for the company's financial health and an indication of what it can and cannot do. Properly done, ratio analysis should permit the general manager to evaluate the financial health of a firm by providing data to answer these three basic questions:

---

8. Different mixes of long term debt and equity can cause the ROE of a firm to vary considerably even though the amount of assets required to support a given level of sales remains unchanged. Thus some managers prefer to divide net income by net assets (the left hand side of the balance sheet) to get the return on net assets, or RONA, which is independent of the amount of debt and equity in the firm's capital structure. RONA may be calculated either pre-tax or after tax. Note that the pre-tax RONA should be very close to ROE for firms where total debt (short plus long term) equals shareholders' equity. This is because pre-tax RONA is about twice net income and total assets are about twice shareholders' equity.

1. *Can the company pay its bills?* A current ratio of 1.5 : 1 or greater and a liquidity ratio of 0.5 : 1 or greater would indicate yes. In contrast, a liquidity ratio less than 0.5 : 1 combined with an increasing average for days payable and a decreasing average for days receivable would indicate a cash problem that requires immediate attention.

2. *Has the company borrowed too much money?* Here the debt to equity ratio can give an indication of potential future borrowing capacity or limitations. All things begin equal, a firm with no long term debt has much greater flexibility to borrow money to take advantage of investment opportunities than does a firm whose debt to equity ratio is above 1 : 1.

3. *How effectively does the company make money?* Some companies struggle along for years making just enough to survive, while others consistently earn more than fifteen percent on their shareholders' equity. Return on equity is the best overall measure of a firm's ability to earn money, but it must be tempered with reason. A firm with very low equity may have an abnormally high return on equity. Due to their capital structure, utilities and finance companies may have a somewhat lower return on equity than most industrial firms. Family businesses may also be misleading since family members may take very high salaries and not care about profitability figures as long as the business breaks even. On the other hand, a very high ROE (30% or more) may indicate that only a small fixed asset base is needed to support a high level of sales (e.g., mobile home builders or retailing firms which lease store space).

The Free cash flow analysis described in Chapter 3 is an excellent supplement to ratio analysis. While Ratio analysis evaluates a firm's financial condition at a point in time, Free cash flow analysis shows how much cash a firm generates over a period of years. Taken together, Ratio analysis and Free cash flow analysis provide a clear picture of a firm's financial condition and its ability to generate cash.

Checking Ratios Against Industry Norms

Sometimes it is desirable to compare a particular ratio to the industry norm for that company. This can be done through use of one of several appropriate reference books such as:

1. Troy, Leo, *Almanac of Business and Industrial Financial Ratios*, current edition. Englewood Cliffs, New Jersey: Prentice-Hall.

2. *Annual Statement Studies*, published by Robert Morris Associates, Credit Division, Philadelphia National Bank Building, Philadelphia, PA 19107.

3. Levine, Sumner, and Caroline Levine, editors. *The Business One Irwin Business & Investment Almanac*, published annually by Richard D. Irwin. A comprehensive review of financial data for the preceding year and an explanation of financial terms.

However, it is always preferable for the general manager to start out with a clear understanding of what the ratios should be in a typically well run firm. Then if significant deviations become apparent, the general manager can ask pertinent questions about a firm's strengths and weaknesses in finance, management, marketing and production as appropriate.

A FORM TO HELP WITH RATIO ANALYSIS

Exhibit 3.1 illustrates the use of a form to help you calculate these ratios and quickly assess a firm's financial health. It has been completed for the Kellogg Company whose 1994 balance sheet and income statement are given in Exhibit 3.2 Inventory includes both Raw materials and supplies and Finished Goods and materials in process. Intangible assets (4.1) and other assets (136.9) were subtracted from total assets (4,467) to get total tangible assets of 4,326. When calculating Payables, only Accounts payable are used. Accounts payable represent debts owed to creditors for goods or services supplied to the firm. Notes payable are not included because they represent an obligation to repay borrowed funds, usually to a bank. Nonpension postretirement benefits are not considered part of long term debt because no interest charges are associated with them. They are similar to deferred taxes, in that they represent a claim on assets to be paid in future time periods. Other liabilities are also treated like Deferred income taxes and are not included as part of long term debt.

Ratio analysis confirms what you may have suspected about this well-known Fortune 500 corporations; it is indeed in good financial health. Appendix A contains a blank copy of this form.

SUMMARY

Ratio analysis is an invaluable way to assess the financial health of a firm quickly and accurately. The nine ratios described in this chapter are applicable to most firms, including small businesses. They are usually sufficient to assess a firm's financial health and spot trends over time, such as a significant increase or decrease in long term debt. When possible, Ratio analysis should be combined with a Free cash flow analysis to get a complete picture of a firm's financial condition and performance over time.

Common Financial Ratios

Company: Kellogg Company		Year: 1994

Ratio (Standard)	Formula		Calculation
Current Ratio (1.5 : 1)	=	$\dfrac{\text{Current Assets}}{\text{Current Liabilities}}$	1.2 $\dfrac{1,433}{1,185}$
Liquidity Ratio (0.5 : 1)	=	$\dfrac{\text{Liquid Current Assets}}{\text{Current Liabilities}}$	0.7 $\dfrac{831}{1,185}$
Receivables (30 days)	=	$\dfrac{\text{Accounts Receivable}}{\text{Sales}} \times 360$	30.9 $\dfrac{564 \times 360}{6,562}$
Payables (30 days)	=	$\dfrac{\text{Accounts Payable}}{\text{Cost of Goods Sold}} \times 360$	40.7 $\dfrac{334 \times 360}{2,951}$
Inventory (days) (30 - 60 days)	=	$\dfrac{\text{Inventory}}{\text{Cost of Goods Sold}} \times 360$	48.3 $\dfrac{396 \times 360}{2,951}$
Debt/Equity (< .5)	=	$\dfrac{\text{Long Term Debt}}{\text{Shareholders' Equity}}$	.40 $\dfrac{719}{1,807}$
Assets/Sales (1 : 1 average)	=	$\dfrac{\text{Total Tangible Assets}}{\text{Sales}}$	.66 $\dfrac{4,326}{6,562}$
Return on Sales (3 - 5% average)	=	$\dfrac{\text{Net Income}}{\text{Sales}}$	10.7% $\dfrac{705 \times 100}{6,562}$
Return on Equity (15% minimum)	=	$\dfrac{\text{Net Income}}{\text{Shareholders' Equity}}$	39.0% $\dfrac{705 \times 100}{1,807}$

A. Three basic questions:

1. Can it pay its bills?   ✓ Yes   ___ No

   Current ratio   =   1.2

   Liquidity ratio   =   0.7

2. Has it borrowed too much money?   ✓ No   ___ Maybe   ___ Yes
                                        < .5   5 - 1.0   > 1.0

   Debt/Equity   =   .40

3. How well does it earn money?   ✓ Very Well   ___ Well   ___OK   ___Poor
                                      > 20%   15-20% 10-15% <10%

   Return on Sales   =   10.7%

   Return on Equity   =   39.0%

B. Overall assessment of financial health   ✓ Excellent ___ Good ___Fair ___Weak

C. Any special factors that should be noted about this firm:

Net income of $705 is almost equal to long term debt of $719.
Excellent return on sales of 10.7%.
Return on equity would not be so high (39%) if Kellogg had not repurchased so many of its shares, which it holds as Treasury stock. If the $1,981 spent on Treasury stock is added to the $1,807 of Shareholders' equity, then return on equity would fall to a more reasonable but still very respectable 22.3%.

Exhibit 3.1. Use of a form to assess the financial health of a company.

Kellogg Company and Subsidiaries
Consolidated Earnings and Retained Earnings
Year ended December 31,

(millions, except per share data)	1994	1993	1992
Net sales	$6,562.0	$6,295.4	$6,190.6
Cost of goods sold	2,950.7	2,989.0	2,987.7
Selling and administrative expense	2,448.7	2,237.5	2,140.1
Operating profit	1,162.6	1,068.9	1,062.8
Interest expense	45.4	33.3	29.2
Other income (expense), net	12.8	(1.5)	36.8
Earnings before income taxes and cumulative effect of accounting change	1,130.0	1,034.1	1,070.4
Income taxes	424.6	353.4	387.6
Earnings before cumulative effect of accounting change	705.4	680.7	682.8
Cumulative effect of change in method of accounting for postretirement benefits other than pensions – $1.05 per share (net of income tax benefit of $144.6)			(251.6)
Net earnings – $3.15, $2.94, $1.81 per share	705.4	680.7	431.2
Retained earnings, beginning of year	3,409.4	3,033.9	2,889.1
Dividends paid – $1.40, $1.32, $1.20 per share	(313.6)	(305.2)	(286.4)
Retained earnings, end of year	$3,801.2	$3,409.4	$3,033.9

See notes to consolidated financial statements.

Kellogg Company and Subsidiaries
Consolidated Balance Sheet
At December 31,

(millions)	1994	1993
Current assets		
Cash and temporary investments	$ 266.3	$ 98.1
Accounts receivable, less allowances of $6.2 and $6.0	564.5	536.8
Inventories:		
Raw materials and supplies	141.7	148.5
Finished goods and materials in process	254.6	254.6
Deferred income taxes	79.4	85.5
Other current assets	127.0	121.6
Total current assets	1,433.5	1,245.1
Property		
Land	47.3	40.6
Buildings	1,122.6	1,065.7
Machinery and equipment	3,141.0	2,857.6
Construction in progress	289.6	308.6
Accumulated depreciation	(1,707.7)	(1,504.1)
Property, net	2,892.8	2,768.4
Intangible assets	4.1	59.1
Other assets	136.9	164.5
Total assets	$ 4,467.3	$ 4,237.1

Exhibit 3.2. Income statement and balance sheet for the Kellogg Company. *Source*: *1994 Kellogg Company Annual Report*, reprinted with permission.

Kellogg Company and Subsidiaries
Consolidated Balance Sheet continued
At December 31,

(millions, except share data)	1994	1993
Current liabilities		
Current maturities of long-term debt	$ .9	$ 1.5
Notes payable	274.8	386.7
Accounts payable	334.5	308.8
Accrued liabilities:		
Income taxes	72.0	65.9
Salaries and wages	80.5	76.5
Advertising and promotion	257.5	233.8
Other	165.0	141.4
Total current liabilities	1,185.2	1,214.6
Long-term debt	719.2	521.6
Nonpension postretirement benefits	486.8	450.9
Deferred income taxes	198.1	188.9
Other liabilities	70.5	147.7
Shareholders' equity		
Common stock, $.25 par value		
Authorized: 330,000,000 shares		
Issued: 310,356,488 shares in 1994 and 310,292,753 in 1993	77.6	77.6
Capital in excess of par value	68.6	72.0
Retained earnings	3,801.2	3,409.4
Treasury stock, at cost: 88,655,238 shares in 1994 and 82,372,409 in 1993	(1,980.6)	(1,653.1)
Minimum pension liability adjustment		(25.3)
Currency translation adjustment	(159.3)	(167.2)
Total shareholders' equity	1,807.5	1,713.4
Total liabilities and shareholders' equity	$ 4,467.3	$ 4,237.1

See notes to consolidated financial statements.

Exhibit 3.2. Continued.

A basic principle of accounting is that income and revenues should be counted in the period in which they occur. The *accrual* method of accounting is based on this principle, and in theory should be the only way to account for income and expenses. In practice the Internal Revenue Service (IRS) allows some modications to the accrual method to simplify the reporting of income and expenses in certain situations (e.g., individuals, small businesses, multi-year contracts). Consequently there are now several sets of accounting rules acceptable to the IRS which may be used for the purposes of computing revenues, expenses and taxes.

The general manager should be familiar with the following four of these methods and know how they differ from each other: the pure cash method, the modified cash method, the accrual method and the long-term contracts method.[1]

1. *The pure cash method.* This means that all transactions take place for cash. There are no accounts receivable and no accounts payable. In practice, almost no business larger than a lemonade stand uses the pure cash method of accounting.
2. *The modified cash method.* Here time of payment, not time of performance, is the governing criterion. Thus revenues and expenses are recorded at the time payment is received for goods sold or services provided, or the day the bills are paid. Gross income includes all items of income *actually received* during the year. Expenses are generally deducted in the tax year in which they were incurred. One exception is expenses paid in advance which can only be deducted in the year to which they apply, such as a three year insurance policy.

The modified cash basis is used by most individuals and many small businesses such as bowling alleys, restaurants or gas stations. A major advantage of the modified cash method is its simplicity in computing annual revenue and expenses. Daily cash receipts and disbursements are also the daily sales and expenses, and annual sales and expenses are simply the sum of daily sales and expenses.

The test of whether a small business can use the modified cash method is whether it is necessary to take inventory into account to accurately compute the cost of goods sold for the year. Cost of goods sold equals starting inventory plus purchases plus work in progress (for a manufacturing firm) less final inventory. A manufacturing firm would have to take into account work in process and the difference between starting and ending finished goods inventory to compute cost of goods sold, and hence could not use the cash method of accounting. On the other hand, a bowling alley or restaurant has little inventory and would be able to use the modified cash method.

---

1. Based on material in *Tax Guide for Small Business*, publication 334 of the Internal Revenue Service.

A second advantage of the modified cash method is that it provides some control over the year in which revenues and expenses are counted for tax purposes. This is particularly true of expenses, where payment of bills may be speeded up or delayed as desired. Thus if a small business knows its sales are going to be unusually high in the current year, it may pay as many bills as possible before the end of the year to reduce its taxes. On the other hand, if a small business expects a much better year next year than this year, it may choose to defer paying bills that could be paid in either year to reduce the next year's burden.

3. *The accrual method.* This method makes a rigorous attempt to match income and expenses to the year in which they are actually incurred. All items of income are included in gross income in the year in which they were earned, even if payment for them is actually received in another tax year. Expenses are also deducted from net income in the year in which incurred, not in the year in which they were actually paid. Here is where inventories become important. If inventories are necessary to accurately compute cost of goods sold, and hence income, then only the accrual basis may be used for purchases and sales.[2] The accrual method is used by most manufacturing businesses and retail establishments.

4. *The long-term contracts method.* A long-term contract is one which takes longer than the standard accounting period of one year to complete. Examples of long-term contracts are construction of a bridge or building, or the fulfillment of a manufacturing contract that is not completed in the tax year in which it started. Income from a long-term contract may be accounted for by either the percentage of completion method or the completed contract method.

    a. Percentage of completion method. Only the portion of the contract price that represents the percentage of the contract completed during the year are deducted. However, to compute the deduction for materials or supplies, add the cost of materials and supplies on hand at the beginning of the year. This method may be considered a way to approximate the accrual method for situations where one year is too short a period of time to account for all transactions.

    b. Completed contract method. Reporting all income and expense items related to the contract is deferred until the year the contract is finally completed and accepted. However, materials and supplies that remain on hand at the end of the contract may not be deducted as expenses. Depreciation and other indirect expenses (such as overhead) must be allocated to specific jobs. The completed contract method may be looked at as a way to artificially create an accounting period greater than one year in length so a long-term contract can be accounted for all at once. For a firm which is engaged in many large projects at a

---

2. Such firms may keep track of inventory through a perpetual inventory system where each time an item is sold the record of stock is automatically updated, often through the use of a computer implemented inventory control system. The system may also be programmed to automatically reorder when stock of an item falls to a certain level. Many businesses (retailers, grocery stores) also count the entire inventory on hand once a year to check the accuracy of the perpetual inventory records.

time, such as Bechtel or Halliburton, the completed contract method will closely approximate the results that would have been attained using the accrual basis.

When a firm undertakes a long-term contract it may receive progress payments which are roughly equal to the percent of the work completed. This helps the contracting firm maintain adequate working capital while work on the contract progresses. Any progress payments received for work done on a long-term contract are accounted for according to the method of accounting elected (either the percentage of completion method or the completed contract method).

THE CASH METHOD IN PRACTICE

The definition of the cash method of accounting is straightforward, but students and business executives alike often have trouble distinguishing it from the accrual method when preparing financial statements. Part of this difficulty stems from confusion in distinguishing between the *pure cash method* of accounting, which can rarely be used in practice, and the *modified cash method* , which is applicable to most individuals and many small businesses. Under the pure cash method, all supplies would be paid for in cash when purchased, all workers would be paid in full at the end of each day, and all sales would be for cash. In such a business there would be no inventory, accounts payable or receivable. As an example of such a business consider Joe, the owner of a hot dog stand near a beach. Assume he buys all of his hot dogs, soft drinks, and other supplies in the morning of each day he is open, and then sells all of them for cash by the end of the day. The balance sheet for a business like Joe's lists cash (including bank balance) as the only short term asset and contains to liabilities (all bills are assumed to be paid the day they are incurred).

In practice most individuals and many small business actually operate on a *modified cash method* of accounting. This means that the pure cash method has been modified to reflect the fact that supplies are not always paid for when received (leading to accounts payable), employees may be paid every two weeks (leading to wages payable) and payment may not be received for services rendered until a later date (leading to accounts receivable). Now the individual may have some accounts receivable as assets and some accounts payable as liabilities. However, as noted earlier, Joe cannot have inventories that are material in determining cost of goods sold.

Assume Joe starts business on January 1 with initial capital contributed of $15,000 and that he uses $10,000 of that money to buy a hot dog stand which he depreciates on a straight line basis over a period of five years. (For purposes of illustration, the half year convention required by MACRS is not used.) His balance sheet on the day he starts business is given in Exhibit 4.1. Now assume that Joe has sales of $50,000 for the year (all received in cash), expenses of $30,000 for supplies (which he paid for in cash when he purchased them) and $8,000 for his helper (whom Joe pays in full at the end of each working day). His income statement for the year now looks as shown in Exhibit 4.2.

Joe's balance sheet at the end of his first year in business is shown in Exhibit 4.3. This is as close to the pure cash method of accounting as a business can come. Note that there are no receivables or liabilities (accounts payable) on the balance sheets in either Exhibits 4.1 or 4.3.

In practice both individuals and small businesses will have some accounts receivable and accounts payable. Thus the pure cash method is commonly modified to reflect the fact that supplies aren't always paid for when received, workers are almost never paid daily and thirty days is usually given customers to pay their bills. Now the individual or business will have some accounts receivable as assets and accounts payable as liabilities at the end of the year which are not counted as income or expenses for that year. Technically this violates the principle of matching revenues and expenses to the period in which they occur. However, the Internal Revenue Service permits these modifications so long as they don't materially (significantly) distort the income and expense statements of the individual or business, and so long as they are consistently applied.[3]

Assets		Liabilities and Owner's Equity		
Cash	$ 5,000	Liabilities		$ 0
Hot dog stand	10,000	Owner's equity		
		Capital contributed	$15,000	
	_____	Retained earnings	—0—	15,000
	$15,000			$15,000

Exhibit 4.1. Balance sheet, Joe's Hot Dog Stand, January 1, 19XX.

Sales			$50,000
Cost of goods sold—supplies	$30,000		
—helper	8,000	$38,000	
Depreciation (20% of $10,000)		2,000	40,000
Gross income			$10,000
Taxes (assume 30% rate, paid as incurred)			3,000
Net income			$7,000

Exhibit 4.2. Income statement for Joe's Hot Dog Stand, 19XX (pure cash method of accounting).

Assets			Liabilities and Owner's Equity		
Cash		$14,000	Liabilities		$ 0
Hot dog stand	$10,000		Owner's equity		
less: accumulated			Capital contributed	$15,000	
depreciation	2,000	8,000	Retained earnings	7,000	22,000
		$22,000			$22,000

Exhibit 4.3. Balance sheet for Joe's Hot Dog Stand at the end of year one (pure cash method of accounting).

---

3. There should be no account for taxes payable. This is because the IRS requires that businesses make estimated tax payments during the year with the last payment due before the end of the business's tax year. At the end of the year, when the exact amount of tax is known, adjusting entries can be made to reflect an additional amount of tax payable or a refund due the company, but in either case the amount should be small.

Assume now that Joe pays his helper every two weeks, orders supplies for a week at a time, is given thirty days to pay his bills and has some good customers whom he bills at the end of each month for the hot dogs they have eaten during the month. His starting balance sheet would be unchanged but now his income statement for the year and his year end balance sheet would reflect these modifications, assumed to be as follows at the end of the year:

- accounts payable: $2,500
  ($27,500 of $30,000 in bills paid, leaving $2,500 still due)
- accounts receivable from customers: $2,000
  ($48,000 of $50,000 billed to customers has been received, leaving $2,000 still due)
- wages payable to helper: $300
  (money earned by helper but not paid as of the end of the year)

Now Joe's income statement for the year would be as shown in Exhibit 4.4 and his balance sheet would be as shown in Exhibit 4.5. The $1,360 difference in cash on hand as shown in the balance sheets in Exhibit 4.3 (the pure cash method) and Exhibit 4.5 (the modified cash method) can be reconciled as shown in Exhibit 4.6.

Thus under the modified cash method Joe would have $1,360 more cash on hand than if he used the pure cash method, the difference between $15,360 under the modified cash method (Exhibit 4.5) and the $14,000 under the pure cash method (Exhibit 4.3). The difference in retained earnings is due to the increase in pre-tax income of $800 ($10,800 – $10,000) less the tax of $240 due on that additional income (30 × $800). Note that if accounts receivable and payable are about equal the modified cash method is a good approximation of the pure cash method in terms of gross income and the amount of tax owed.

Sales			$ 48,000
Cost of goods sold: supplies	$ 27,500		
helper	7,700	$35,200	
Depreciation		2,000	37,200
Gross income			$ 10,800
Taxes (assume 30% of gross income)			3,240
Net income			$ 7,560

Exhibit 4.4. Income statement for Joe's Hot Dog Stand (modified cash basis).

Assets			Liabilities and Owner's Equity		
Cash		$15,360	Accounts payable		$ 2,500
Accounts receivable		2,000	Wages due helper		300
		17,360			$ 2,800
			Owner's equity		
Hot dog stand	$ 10,000				
less: accumulated			Capital contributed	$15,000	
depreciation	2,000	8,000	Retained earnings	7,560	22,560
		$ 25,360			$ 25,360

Exhibit 4.5. Balance sheet for Joe's Hot Dog Stand, December 31, 19XX (modified cash basis).

Transaction (all figures in $)	Change in Cash
Increase in accounts payable (2,500 – 0)	$ 2,500
Increase in wages due helper (300 – 0)	300
Increase in retained earnings (7,560 – 7,000)	560
	$3,360
Less:	
Increase in accounts receivable (2,000 – 0)	2,000
Change (increase) in cash	$1,360

Exhibit 4.6. Reconciliation of change in cash between Exhibits 4.3 and 4.5.

GOING TO THE ACCRUAL METHOD

It's now as small step to go from the modified cash basis to the accrual basis of accounting. The only difference is that the *full amounts* of both revenues and expenses are accounted for on the income statement in the year in which they were incurred, not necessarily when they were paid. Under the accrual method, the income statement would look as shown in Exhibit 4.7 and the balance sheet as shown in Exhibit 4.8

Sales			$ 50,000
Cost of goods sold: supplies	$ 30,000		
helper	8,000	$38,000	
Depreciation		2,000	40,000
Gross income			$ 10,000
Taxes (assume 30% of gross income)			3,000
Net income			$ 7,000

Exhibit 4.7. Income statement for Joe's Hot Dog Stand, 19XX (accrual basis).

Assets			Liabilities and Owner's Equity		
Cash		$14,800	Accounts payable		$ 2,500
Accounts receivable		2,000	Wages due helper		300
		16,800			$ 2,800
			Owner's equity		
Hot dog stand	$ 10,000				
less: accumulated			Capital contributed	$15,000	
depreciation	2,000	8,000	Retained earnings	7,560	22,000
		$ 24,800			$ 24,800

Exhibit 4.8. Balance sheet for Joe's Hot Dog Stand, December 31, 19XX (accrual basis).

The differences between the pure cash, the modified cash, and the accrual methods of accounting are summarized below.

1. Accrual method compared to pure cash method.
   a. The *income statement* is the same as under the pure cash method (revenues and expenses are counted when they occur)
   b. The *balance sheets* differ in that there are receivables and payables on the balance sheet using the accrual method where there are none under the pure cash method.
2. Accrual method compared to modified cash method.
   a. The *income statements* are slightly different, because under the modified cash method the only revenues or expenses recognized are those for which cash payment has been received or made during the reporting period.
   b. The balance sheets are identical with two exceptions:
      (1) retained earnings may differ due to the differences in net income between the two methods
      (2) cash may differ due to the slight differences in taxes resulting from the different net incomes under the two methods.

EVALUATING MERCHANDISE INVENTORY

Retailing firms have some choice in the way they value their inventory. If a firm chooses the LIFO method, described below, it will have an entry either on the balance sheet or in the accompanying notes having to do with *LIFO reserve*. The meaning of this odd-sounding entry will become clear when we review the four basic methods of evaluating merchandise inventory in retailing firms.[4]

4. For a more complete discussion, see, for example, Roger H. Hermanson and James Don Edwards, *Financial Accounting: A Business Perspective*, sixth edition (Chicago, IL: Irwin, 1995), chapters 6 and 7.

1. Specific identification. This method attaches a cost to each identifiable unit of inventory. This is quite logical for one of a kind items, such as autos or real estate, but is impractical for large mass merchandisers.

2. First in, first out (FIFO). FIFO costing assumes that the costs of the first goods purchased are those used when calculating cost of goods sold. FIFO is the logical choice when the first units in (dairy products, vegetables) should be the first units sold. FIFO is easy to apply. The balance sheet amount for inventory is also likely to approximate the current market value, since the last units received are assumed to be the ones in inventory. However, in times of rising prices, FIFO leads to higher profit per unit, and consequently higher taxes, since each unit sold is assumed to be the first unit purchased, probably at a lower price than for the equivalent item at market prices.

3. Last in, first out (LIFO). LIFO assumes that the most recent purchases are the first costs charged to cost of goods sold when product is sold. Compared to FIFO, LIFO leads to lower taxes in periods of rising prices. However, LIFO can substantially understate the current value of inventory, since the items remaining in inventory were probably purchased at lower prices.

4. Weighted average. This method uses a weighted-average unit cost to find the cost of ending inventory. This method is applicable for units that are basically the same, such as toys, books or hardware items, but may have been purchased at different prices.

Lower-of-cost-or-market. Accountants often employ another rule, lower-of-cost-or-market (LCM), which may be used with any of the four inventory valuation methods just discussed. LCM is an inventory costing method that values inventory at the lower of its historical cost or its current market (replacement) cost. Under LCM, inventory items are written down to market value when the market value is less than the cost of the items. If a loss occurs due to the writedown, it is taken in the period in which it occurs.

The Internal Revenue Service permits firms to elect LIFO for tax purposes, but if they do, *they must also use LIFO for financial reporting* (e.g., in annual reports). In a large firm, there can be a significant difference in the value of inventory under FIFO (which approximates market value) and LIFO (which can considerably understate the value of inventory). Some retail firms, such as The Limited, use FIFO. Both Dayton-Hudson and Wal-Mart Stores use LIFO, but they report their results differently. Dayton-Hudson gives a single figure for inventory ($2,497,000,000 on January 29, 1994) and provides further information in this note:

> Inventories and the related cost of sales are accounted for by the retail inventory accounting method using the last-in, first-out (LIFO) basis. The accumulated LIFO provision was $80 million and $171 million at year-end 1993 and 1992, respectively.

In its 1995 Annual Report, Wal-Mart shows the difference between LIFO valuation of inventory and market value directly on its balance sheet.

	(figures in millions)	
	1994	**1995**
Inventories		
At replacement cost	$ 14,415	$ 11,483
less LIFO reserve	351	469
LIFO	$ 14,064	$ 11,014

The LIFO reserve is the amount by which the LIFO method understates the market value of inventory. If the company sold all of its inventory at replacement cost, it would incur a gain equal to the LIFO reserve.

It is more accurate to calculate the days inventory ratio using the replacement cost figure, but if the LIFO reserve is small, there will be little difference in the figures.

Inventory procedures are similar for manufacturing firms, but those firms also have raw materials inventory and work in process inventory as well as finished goods inventory, making the calculations somewhat more complex. A discussion of manufacturing inventory techniques can be found in most texts on cost accounting.

SUMMARY

This chapter has reviewed the four basic ways the IRS allows businesses to account for income and expenses. It has also used the simple example of a hot dog stand owner to show the differences between three of the methods; the pure cash, the modified cash and the accrual methods. The fourth method, the long-term contract method, is applicable only to firms which have long term contracts. Both the pure cash and the accrual methods attempt to match expenses and revenues to the period in which they occur, a basic principle of managerial accounting. But because the pure cash method is so difficult to implement in practice, the IRS permits use of the modified cash method for businesses which do not have significant inventories. (Business owners who say they use the cash method of accounting almost always mean that they are using the modified cash method of accounting.) The accrual method is used by virtually all large corporations.

The following guidance is offered in selecting an accounting method:

1. The *pure cash method* can't be used if the business has any receivables or payables at all. This eliminates almost all businesses.
2. The *modified cash method* can be used as long as inventories do not play a material role in calculating cost of goods sold and hence net income. This requirement eliminates the modified cash method for virtually all manufacturing and retail businesses. It is primarily used by individuals and small service businesses. Its primary advantage is simplicity in bookkeeping to determine gross sales and cost of goods sold. Gross sales equal the sum of payments received less any returns, and cost of goods sold equals the sum of cash receipts for expenses.

3. The *long-term contracts* method is applicable to businesses which have contracts that last more than a year.
4. The *accrual* basis must be used by all other businesses.

Financial leverage is the use of funds for a prolonged period (such as long term debt) for which the firm pays a fixed cost (interest charges) in hopes of increasing the return to the common shareholders. Positive or favorable leverage results when the firm earns more with the additional funds than the fixed cost of those funds (i.e., the interest charges). Negative or unfavorable leverage results when the firm does not earn as much on the additional funds as the fixed cost of those funds. Tax considerations are also important, since interest charges associated with borrowing money are a deductible expense when computing taxes.

The effects of using financial leverage are reflected on both the balance sheet and the income statement. When a firm is highly leveraged, its balance sheet will show a high ratio of long term debt to shareholders' equity and substantial interest charges as an expense on the income statement. These interest charges are directly proportional both to how much is borrowed and the rate of interest charged. The higher the interest rate that must be paid, the less desirable leverage becomes.[1] A firm with no long term debt (and hence no interest charges) has no financial leverage associated with it.

ATTRACTION OF LEVERAGE

The great attraction of financial leverage is that when times are good, the shareholders receive a proportionately greater return from their investment in the form of higher earnings per share.[2] However, leverage is a two-edged sword; when times are bad, shareholders share disproportionately in reductions in earnings per share as well. These effects can be demonstrated by an example. Assume that XYZ Company desires to raise an additional $10,000,000 to take advantage of a promising opportunity to manufacture and market a new product.

Assume further that three financing plans are under consideration, recognizing that in reality an infinite number of variations of these plans could be devised.

- *Plan A* would sell 500,000 new shares of common stock at $20 per share to raise the $10,000,000

---

1. A similar effect can be obtained using preferred stock, which has a fixed dividend rate. Unlike the interest charges associated with long term debt, dividends on preferred stock are not deductible as an expense when computing taxes. Preferred stock is frequently used by utilities as an alternative to issuing long term debt and by firms exchanging stock in the form of a convertible preferred issue (one that can be converted to a specified number of shares of common stock at a predetermined price) when acquiring another firm.
2. Leverage is a concept borrowed from physics whereby a long stick or lever is used to move an object that is too heavy to be moved otherwise.

- *Plan B* would raise half the money from the sale of new common stock and half from issuing long term debt; and
- *Plan C* would raise all the money from issuing long term debt.

For purposes of demonstration, assume that the interest rate on the long term debt is 10%, the tax rate is 50%, earnings before interest and taxes (EBIT) are $3,000,000, and that the XYZ Company presently has 500,000 shares of common stock outstanding. The effect on *earnings per share* of each of these financing plans is shown in Exhibit 5.1.

	Plan A (all stock)	Plan B (50% stock; 50% debt)	Place C (all debt)
Original stock	$10,000,000	$10,000,000	$10,000,000
Add'l stock @ $ 20/share	10,000,000	5,000,000	–0–
Debt at 10%	–0–	5,000,000	10,000,000
Total funding	$20,000,000	$20,000,000	$20,000,000
Assume EBIT (earnings before interest and taxes of $3,000,000			
EBIT	$3,000,000	$3,000,000	$3,000,000
Interest @ 10%	–0–	500,000	1,000,000
Earnings before taxes	3,000,000	2,500,000	2,000,000
Taxes (50%)	1,500,000	1,250,000	1,000,000
Earnings	$ 1,500,000	$ 1,250,000	$ 1,000,000
Previous shares	500,000	500,000	500,000
Additional shares	500,000	250,000	–0–
Total shares	1,000,000	750,000	500,000
Earnings per share	$ 1.50	$ 1.67	$ 2.00

Exhibit 5.1. Three financing plans for the XYZ Company.

In the situation in Exhibit 5.1, times are basically good. The $3,000,000 in earnings before interest and taxes is considerably more than the interest charges incurred. This is true even in Plan C where debt is used to raise all of the additional $10,000,000. As we would expect in such circumstances, earnings per share (although not total earnings) are greatest under Plan C. Assuming for the moment that dividends (which, if paid, would be subtracted from the earnings per share figure in Exhibit 5.1) and market price per share are directly related to earnings per share, then shareholders should prefer and benefit most from financing Plan C.[3]

---

3. Earnings before interest and taxes (EBIT) in Exhibit 5.1 are $3,000,000 which is s 30% return on the new funding of $10,000,000. Since this rate is greater that the 10% interest for debt, there will be a net gain in earnings. However, if the earnings before interest and taxes were only $2,000,000 there would be *no difference* in earnings per share in Plans A, B or C. This is because the firm is only earning 10% before interest and taxes, exactly the same as the rate of interest it is paying to borrow the additional funds. In this unique case, there would be no leverage effect, either good or bad. This can be demonstrated by using a figure of EBIT of $2,000,000 rather than $6,000,000 in Exhibit 5.1 and redoing subsequent calculations. Earnings per share will be $1.00 in each case.

To further illustrate the favorable aspects of leverage in good times, assume that next year the new product sells well and that earnings before interest and taxes (EBIT) doubles from $3,000,000 to $6,000,000. The effects are shown in Exhibit 5.2. Note that in Plans B and C where leverage (i.e., debt) is used earnings per share *more than double* when earnings before interest and taxes are doubled from $3,000,000 to $3,000,000. Under Plan A, where no debt is used (and hence there is no leverage), earnings per share increase by the *same percentage* (100%) that earnings before interest and taxes increase.

	Plan A (all stock)	Plan B (50% stock; 50% debt)	Place C (all debt)
EBIT	$6,000,000	$6,000,000	$6,000,000
Interest @ 10%	–0–	500,000	1,000,000
Earnings before taxes	6,000,000	5,500,000	5,000,000
Taxes (50%)	3,000,000	2,750,000	2,500,000
Earnings	$ 3,000,000	$ 2,750,000	$ 2,500,000
Previous shares	500,000	500,000	500,000
Additional shares	500,000	250,000	–0–
Total shares	1,000,000	750,000	500,000
Earnings per share	$ 3.00	$ 3.66	$ 5.00
% increase in EPS over EPS in Exhibit 5.1	+ 100%	+ 120%	+ 150%

Exhibit 5.2. Favorable leverage.

PUNITIVE EFFECTS

Now consider the opposite situation. The new product is not a success, and earnings before interest and taxes fall to zero. The punitive effects of leverage in bad times are show in Exhibit 5.3. Under the conservative, unleveraged Plan A, the shareholders certainly don't do well, but they don't suffer a loss, either. Under Plans B and C, both of which utilize leverage, matters are much worse since the interest charges must be paid whether or not earnings before interest and taxes are positive. Under Plan B there is a loss per share of $.67; under Plan C, which uses even more debt, the loss increases to $2.00 per share.

This example emphasizes the two-edged nature of leverage: any change in earnings before interest and taxes produces an exaggerated effect, good or bad, on earnings per share when long term debt (leverage) rather than equity is used to finance the business. Any firm that loses money year in and year out will eventually go bankrupt. However, a highly leveraged firm is more likely to go bankrupt sooner than a firm whose long term financing is all in the form of equity because legally the interest charges on the loan must still be paid.[4]

---

4. One of the advantages of using all common stock to finance growth is that the firm has no similar legal obligation to pay dividends and can elect not to pay them in bad times to conserve cash.

	Plan A (all stock)	Plan B (50% stock; 50% debt)	Place C (all debt)
EBIT	–0–	–0–	–0–
Interest @ 10%	–0–	$ 500,000	$ 1,000,000
Earnings before taxes	–0–	(500,000)	(1,000,000)
Taxes (50%)	–0–	–0–	–0–
Earnings	–0–	$ (500,000)	$ (1,000,000)
Common shares	100,000	750,000	500,000
Earnings per share	$ –0–	$ (0.67)	$(2.00)
	( ) means a negative number or a loss		

Exhibit 5.3. Effects of leverage when EBIT is zero.

EVALUATION OF LEVERAGE

How much leverage is enough? How much is too much? These are difficult questions to answer because different industries and economic environments have different levels of risk associated with them. While one firm may choose not to incur any long term debt another may borrow as long as funds are available at a reasonable rate.

Here are three reasons why some firms have chosen not to incur any long term debt (i.e., no leverage):

1. Management philosophy. Wary of leverage's ill effects in bad times, management simply decides to rule out the use of long term debt.
2. Debt not needed. For a fortunate few firms, cash generation from earnings and depreciation is sufficient to fund the desired level. Hewlett-Packard, Dun & Bradstreet, Liz Claiborne and Microsoft are familiar examples of firms with little or no long term debt.
3. Bad credit rating. A firm's credit rating may not be good enough to convince a bank to loan it money on a long term basis. This is particularly likely to be true of small or newly established businesses.

Despite these reasons for not incurring long term debt, most firms incur at least some long term debt. Here are three reasons why:

1. Asset intensiveness. Firms in some businesses are not able to acquire sufficient assets without extensive borrowing. Examples include airlines, utilities and leasing companies. If the revenues are likely to be steady, as from customers for an electric utility, then there may be comparatively little risk associated with incurring unusually large amounts of long term debt.
2. Accelerate growth. Management may feel it is wise to use leverage (i.e., borrow money) to accelerate the rate of growth of a firm. Carl Gerstacker of Dow Chemical Company is given much of

the credit for pioneering this "responsible use of debt" concept to accelerate plant construction in the 1950's and make Dow a world class chemical company. The wisdom of Gerstacker's decisions is evident in retrospect. The cost to replace the plants that Dow built in the 1950's and 1960's when interest rates were less than five percent would be many times higher today. More recently, Marriott Corporation has borrowed heavily to accelerate the rate at which it builds hotels. In 1990 Marriott's debt to equity ratio was just over 6:1.

3. Not dilute equity. McDonald's Corporation chose to issue debt rather than sell additional shares of stock to finance its rapid expansion in the 1960's and 1970's to preserve the equity position of the original shareholders. If additional shares had been issued, net income would have been spread over these additional shares when computing earnings per share. As Richard Boylan, who was in charge of McDonald's finances in the 1970's, stated, "By borrowing, you lock in a rate and eventually pay off the loan. But you are never through paying for an equity financing [sale of stock], because the dilution of the stock is permanent and you pay dividends on the new shares forever."[5]

SUMMARY

The most important point about leverage is that management should know what it is getting into when it changes the capital structure by taking on long term debt and thus subjecting the firm to the effects of leverage. There are reasonable and responsible uses of debt, but just as in personal life, borrowing too much money often results in trouble in the long run.[6] There is also an opportunity cost involved. Once a firm has borrowed to its capacity, it loses its ability to borrow in the future, and as a consequence may not be able to take advantage of attractive business opportunities that may arise.

---

5. John F. Love, *McDonald's: Behind the Arches* (New York: Bantam Books, 1986), p. 286.
6. Recall from Chapter 1 that as a conservative guideline long term debt should not exceed one-half of shareholders' equity in a large firm.

In this chapter we turn to a discussion of concepts which relate the accounting and financial terms discussed thus far to the *market price* of a share of common stock. The price at which a share of stock sells reflects what someone is willing to pay for that stock at that particular moment, and nothing more.[1] Taken alone, market price tells little about a firm's future prospects or its underlying financial strength. However, when related to such readily obtainable financial and accounting data as earnings per share and return on equity, it can provide managers and investors alike with useful information about the financial status of the firm.

Stock in a firm is generally purchased in the expectation that the firm will prosper (i.e., sales, earnings and dividends will increase) and that the value of the stock will appreciate over time. While two people should get the same answers when they calculate the common financial ratios discussed in Chapter 3 for a particular stock, they may have very different opinions on how much they would pay to own a share of that stock. The old Kentucky saying, "A difference of opinion makes for good horse trading," applies equally well when buying or selling shares of stock.

How does a stock get listed on a national stock exchange? Usually there are several steps which may take years to complete, but many firms have succeeded. Today there are over 4,000 listed common stocks in the United States alone.

FROM SMALL BUSINESS TO PUBLICLY TRADED FIRM

All large, publicly listed companies once started as a small business. Indeed, historically about 90 percent of all businesses in the United States are small (fewer than 100 employees) and owned by an individual (sole proprietor) or a small group of people, either as a partnership or a corporation. Many law firms, public accounting firms and management consulting firms are partnerships because of the tax advantages of this form of organization.[2]

Once a business grows to a certain size (a million dollars in sales is a good dividing line), the owners usually incorporate. That is, they form a corporation where ownership is reflected in terms of

---

1. This assumes the transaction is made through a stockbroker who executes a buy or sell order on a stock exchange. While rarely done, it is quite proper and legal for any two parties to buy and sell stock at a mutually agreeable price without using a broker. Once payment has been made the stock certificate is endorsed by the seller and then sent directly to the company's stock transfer agent, usually a bank so listed on the certificate, to effect transfer of title to the new owner.

2. There are different tax rates for corporations and partnerships. The maximum corporate tax rate is presently 34%, while partnerships are taxed like individuals, whose maximum tax rate is presently 28%. However, a corporation provides substantial protection in terms of liability, while a partner is liable for *all* the debts incurred by his or her fellow partners. An S corporation (or subchapter S, as it is often called) provides the legal protection of a corporation and the tax advantages of partnership, but must meet certain restrictions, including the following: a maximum of 35 stockholders, all of whom must be U.S. citizens or residents, and only one class of stock. Most S corporations are family businesses or new businesses.

shares of stock held. Initially the founders of a business will hold most, if not all, of the stock. There are two main advantages to incorporating:

1. Limited liability. The individual who owns stock is not personally liable for the debts of any other shareholder, or the corporation as a whole. The individual's down-side risk is limited; at worst, his shares of stock will become worthless.
2. Greater liquidity. Shares of stock in a publicly held and traded company can be sold quickly. A partner's share of a partnership offers no such liquidity.

As a corporation continues to grow, it often strives to have its stock listed on a stock exchange to facilitate trading in its shares. If the price of the stock rises, it may be desirable to issue additional shares, a common way for new companies to raise funds to augment working capital or to undertake expansion. Usually a firm is listed on a regional or over-the-counter exchange before being listed on the New York Stock Exchange.[3] The New York Stock Exchange has the most stringent listing requirements and, perhaps because of this, is the most prestigious.[4] However, any of over 3,000 stocks listed in the *Wall Street Journal*'s financial pages can usually be bought or sold with little difficulty, provided the amounts involved are not excessive with respect to the number of shares outstanding.

The National Association of Securities Dealers Automated Quotation System (known as "NAS-DAQ" and pronounced nas-dak'), started in 1971, handles quotations nationwide on over 2,000 over-the-counter stocks, making a ready market for many smaller firms. The NASDAQ also includes some of the country's fastest growing firms, including Microsoft (computer software), Stryker (medical equipment) and Netscape (access to the Internet).

As a firm shifts from a sole proprietorship or a partnership to a publicly traded corporation, the method of evaluating its worth also changes. In the case of a proprietorship or partnership, the buyer and seller agree between themselves on the value of the entire business, including such intangible factors as location and reputation. This is a fairly subjective procedure. Exhibit 6.1 shows one procedure for establishing the value for a small business. The final price, of course, is what the buyer agrees to pay the seller.

Once a firm becomes listed on the NASDAQ or the New York Stock Exchange, ownership is almost always effectively divorced from management. For example, no one owns as much as 5% of the 755 million shares of General Motors Corporation or the 1.2 billion shares of Exxon. Indeed, ownership of as little as 10% of a New York Stock Exchange company is usually enough to effectively control the company. The value of a share of stock, representing ownership in the company, is established by transactions (buy and sell orders) executed on a stock exchange, usually by a registered

---

3. Two exceptions are Compaq Computer Company, maker of personal computers, and Standard Federal Bancorp (of Detroit), both of which were listed directly on the New York Stock Exchange after their initial public stock offerings.
4. General criteria for listing on the New York Stock Exchange are (1) publicly held shares totalling 1,100,000 or more; (2) more than 2,000 holders of 100 or more shares; and (3) aggregate market value of publicly held shares exceeds $18,000,000. If these conditions fail to be met, the stock may be delisted.

stockbroker. The important point here is that the market price per share of stock does not reflect management's evaluation of the value of that share. Rather it reflects what someone is willing to pay for a share of that stock at a particular moment. In contrast, when a small business is sold, it reflects a judgment of the value of the entire business, and ownership (control of the firm) actually changes hands.

1	Book value[a]		$ 500,000
	Adjustments—appreciation of property	150,000	
	—write down of equipment	(50,000)	100,000
	Adjusted book value		$ 600,000
	The adjusted book value represents what the business is worth in terms of its assets alone. If the business is very profit-able, the following steps can be used to determine how much premium (goodwill) to pay;		
2	Present annual after tax earnings	80,000	
3	Desired annual after tax earnings (assume 10% of adjusted book value)	60,000	
4	Annual after tax earnings above desired amount (line 2 minus line 3)	20,000	
5	Amount of goodwill purchaser is willing to pay (excess of pur-chase price over adjusted book value)		100,000
	The $100,000 figure used here is obtained by assuming the buyer wants to recover the amount paid for goodwill in five years, then multiplying five years by the acquired business's annual profitability in excess of the buyer's initial require-ments (already calculated on line four). In practice, this fig-ure will be what the buyer and seller agree upon.		
6	Total value or selling price of business, including a premium over the value of its assets for its high profitability		$700,000
	[a]Book value = Total assets – All liabilities = Shareholders' equity		

Exhibit 6.1. Procedure to estimate the value or selling price of a small business.

TERMS RELATED TO A STOCK'S PRICE

With this background, we will now review the definitions of some terms related to the market price of a share of stock:

1. *Price per share.* This is what it would cost an investor to buy a single share of stock. Brokerage fees are not included in the price per share and generally run about one percent of the total transaction amount. Fees may be lower if a discount brokerage firm is used.
2. *Earnings per share (EPS).* The total earnings of the firm (after taxes but before common stock dividends) divided by the total number of shares outstanding. If there has been a change in the

number of shares outstanding during the year, the average number of shares outstanding is often used.

3. *Price / earnings ratio (P/E)*. The ratio of the price of a share of stock to the earnings per share. Stated conversely, the price of a share of stock equals the earnings per share times the price / earnings ratio. Price / earnings ratios cannot be negative. If a firm has a loss, it has an undefined price / earnings ratio. The price / earnings ratio may also be found by dividing a stock's market value by its total earnings. Market value is equal to price per share times number of shares of stock outstanding.

4. *Dividends*. Many firms pay cash dividends quarterly. Most large firms have a policy of paying about half of their earnings out each year in dividends. The percent of earnings per share paid as dividends is called the *payout ratio*. Growth companies often elect to pay a smaller amount out in dividends, and some companies such as Hewlett-Packard or Microsoft intentionally pay little or no dividends because they have so many attractive internal investment opportunities. Note that a firm can generate enough cash to pay a dividend even if it has a negative net income if its cash flow (net income plus depreciation) is positive. Caterpillar, the maker of earth moving equipment, showed a loss of $0.67 per share in 1991, yet was able to pay a dividend of $0.60 per share to its shareholders out of cash flow of $2.31 per share that year. (Caterpillar did feel the effects of the loss. It reduced its dividend to $0.30 the following year when it showed an even larger loss as a consequence of the then deeply depressed construction equipment market.)

5. *Stock splits and stock dividends*. Investors love to get a stock split or a stock dividend, but often they don't understand what they are getting. When the price per share of a stock gets high (e.g., over $100), many people are reluctant to buy it because its price seems so high. They feel more comfortable buying 100 shares of a twenty-five dollar stock than twenty-five shares of a hundred dollar stock. To reduce the price per share of their stock, firms may declare a *stock split* whereby they give additional shares, or fractions of shares for each share held.[5] A two for one stock split should cause the price of a stock to fall to exactly half its pre-split value since the number of shares outstanding is exactly double. The dividend is reduced accordingly, unless the board of directors also acts to raise the dividend on the split shares.

A *stock dividend* may be viewed as a special kind of stock split. It represents giving a small fraction of a share (one tenth or one twentieth are common amounts) for each share held in lieu of a cash dividend. Some people who receive stock dividends think, incorrectly, that this gives them a greater share of ownership in the company. Since all shareholders receive the same percentage of additional shares, the overall ownership percentage is unchanged by the stock dividend. What has changed is that there are now more shares of the stock outstanding. The price of the stock should also decrease, since the total value of the company has not changed but is now spread over more shares. Theoretically,

---

5.   In practice, fractional shares are not issued. If a 4 for 3 split is declared, an individual owning 100 shares would be given 33 additional shares plus the option to receive cash for the remaining 1/3 share, or to pay enough additional money which, when combined with the 1/3 share, would purchase a full share.

Price per share after split   =

$$\text{Price per share after split} = \frac{\text{Price per share before split}}{1 + \text{Shares received for each share held before the split}}$$

There is, however, a non-financial benefit to stock splits and stock dividends: they make most people feel good when they are declared, even if their percentage ownership in the firm isn't increased.[6]

6. *Book value.* This is net worth per share. It is also what a firm is theoretically worth if it pays all its bills and declares a final liquidating dividend.[7] It can be computed by dividing shareholders' equity by total shares outstanding.

When a firm's book value is substantially above the price of a share of stock, some investors think this is a sign of a "good buy". They reason that if all the stock of a firm selling below book value could be purchased, the debt paid off, and the remaining assets sold at their stated value (this is rarely a good assumption), then a terminating dividend per share greater than the price per share could be declared. In other words, it would be in the best interests of the shareholders to liquidate the firm and invest their funds elsewhere. But keep in mind that a market value well below book value could mean the future prospects of the company simply are not very bright, or the assets are overvalued on the balance sheet.

Sometimes book value is used to refer to net worth, rather than net worth per share, as when evaluating a small business. Whether the amount is per share or not should be evident from the context in which the phrase book value is used.

Two terms that aren't important to know, but which can cause considerable confusion because of their connotations, are *par value* and *capitalization*. Par value is an anachronistic term dating back to the nineteenth century. The major provision of the par value was that dividends could not be paid out of it. Today most states require a minimal par value for stocks of firms incorporating in them (the minimum in Michigan is $1.00) and many require no par value. For practical purposes a stock's par value can be ignored; it is there to meet a legal requirement only.

Capitalization has two meanings. First, it can mean the mix of bonds, preferred stock and equity used to finance a firm's assets. Usually this implies that the cash provided by the financing will be

---

6. There is also a technical difference between a stock split and a stock dividend. When a stock split occurs, the par value is adjusted accordingly so that the value of capital contributed remains the same. When a stock dividend is declared the par value of the stock remains the same. This is because a stock dividend is effectively a purchase of new stock at market price from the company by the shareholder with the amount of his or her dividend. The corporation's capital contributed account must be increased by the amount of the stock dividend. This is important only in that by law in some states dividends cannot be declared out of capital contributed, and a firm giving frequent stock dividends could limit its ability to pay cash dividends.

7. The assumption is that current assets, including inventory, are sufficient to pay off all liabilities, including long term debt. All that would then be left are fixed assets, which are assumed to be sold for cash at their stated value so that the only asset left is cash. Book value per share is this amount of cash divided by shares outstanding.

used to buy long term assets (land, plant and equipment) and supplies which in turn will be used to produce the firm's products.

■ XYZ Company was capitalized half with bonds and half with equity.

Second, it can mean the aggregate market value of a firm's stock, which is its price per share times number of shares outstanding.

■ The capitalization of Wal-Mart of $50 billion makes it virtually immune to takeover.

Capitalization does *not* refer to the process of raising capital or to the economic system known as capitalism.

Often the market price of a share of a company's stock is of more interest to the investor than it is to the managers of the firm. This is because the managers and the shareholders have different perspectives on the value of a firm's stock. Both would naturally like to see the price of a share of stock rise over time. However, while the daily operations of a firm rarely change in response to market fluctuations in its stock, a drop in the price of stock may cause the investor to sell to avoid further losses. The assets of a firm do not fluctuate with the price of its stock, while those of a shareholder do. Always remember that the real value of a share of stock is what someone will pay for it. It is established by many factors outside the control of the firm's management. And some—perhaps most—of these may be emotional and irrational in nature.

SOURCES OF DATA ON STOCKS

The *Wall Street Journal* is the most available and most widely read source of financial data on publicly traded stocks and bonds. Exhibit 6.2 shows what a sample entry for the Kellogg Company looks like in the *Wall Street Journal* and explains the column headings.[8] Of all the data given about a stock in the *Wall Street Journal* or other newspaper, only its P/E ratio and its dividend yield can be meaningfully compared to similar measures about other stocks.[9]

---

8. The *Wall Street Journal* is not published on Saturdays, Sundays or national holidays. However, most general circulation newspapers will provide a daily (including weekend) listing of at least some of the more widely held stocks in its financial section. Detailed statistics are given in *Barron's* or the *Wall Street Transcript*, each published weekly. Daily transactions may also be viewed on television through services such as the Financial News Network.

9. This is because the P/E ratio and dividend yield (also a ratio) express a relationship between two facts about the firm (price per share and earnings per share, for example) and hence are independent of the number of shares outstanding and the total earnings of the firm. To see that this is so, assume the XYZ Company declares a two for one stock split. The earnings per share and dividends per share are both divided by two and the value of each share after the split should be half the value of a share prior to the split. However, the P/E ratio and dividend yield are unchanged. Hence, the number of shares outstanding, stock splits and stock dividends have *no effect* on the P/E ratio or the dividend yield of a firm. Thus ratios such as the P/E ratio and dividend yield of various stocks may be meaningfully compared while facts such as price per share, earnings per share and dividend per share may not.

WAYS TO INCREASE EARNINGS PER SHARE

Earnings per share (EPS) is perhaps the most widely watched barometer of a firm's performance. Indeed, increasing earnings per share is often stated as a primary objective of top management. The most straightforward way to increase earnings per share is to increase earnings while holding the number of shares of stock issued constant. Management may seek to grow (and hence increase earnings) by gaining a larger share of existing markets, entering new markets, developing new products, or some combination thereof. A firm's corporate strategy often indicates how the goal of growth in earnings (and hence in earnings per share) is to be achieved.

However, the general manager should also know that there are two other ways to increase earnings per share, each dealing primarily with the firm's financial policies rather than its corporate strategies.

52 Weeks					Yield			Vol				Net
Hi	Lo	Stock	Sym	Div	%	PE	100s	Hi	Lo	Close	Chg
73 7/8	52 1/2	Kellogg	K	1.56	2.2	22	2829	70 3/8	69 1/2	70 1/8	+ 5/8

Explanation of column headings (all per share), from left to right:

Hi	Highest price paid for Kellogg stock the past 52 weeks.
Lo	Lowest price paid for Kellogg stock the past 52 weeks.
Stock	Name of the company (Kellogg).
Sym	Trading symbol for Kellogg common stock.
Div	Current annual dividend payment in dollars.
Yld %	Annual yield of the stock, expressed in percent. Equals the annual dividend payment divided by the price.
PE	The price-earnings ratio. The price per share divided by the earnings per share for the four most recent quarters.
Vol 100s	Approximate number of shares of stock which exchange hands during trading, expressed in 100s.
Hi	High trade price for Kellogg stock on August 11, 1995.
Lo	Low trade price for Kellogg stock on August 11, 1995.
Close	Last trade price for Kellogg stock on August 11, 1995.
Net Chg	Net change from the close of trading on August 10, 1995 for Kellogg stock.

Note: Earnings per share can be obtained by dividing price per share by the price/earnings ratio. For Kellogg, the earnings per share are equal to $3.18 ($70 1/8 ÷ 22).

Exhibit 6.2. Listing for the Kellogg Company, August 11, 1995.

Buy Back Shares

What can a firm do with its earnings? The usual answers are to pay dividends to shareholders or to reinvest the earnings in attractive growth opportunities within the firm so the earnings will be even larger in the future. Those familiar with finance know there is a third answer: buy back your own company's shares. This has three important effects, all usually good:

a.   a *reduction* in the number of shares outstanding

b.   a *reduction* in the total amount paid in dividends (the dividends per share remain the same, however)

c.   an *increase* in the earnings per share because the earnings from operations, which remain unchanged, are divided by a smaller number of shares outstanding. The only income foregone is interest that would have been earned on the funds used to buy back the shares.

By buying back its own shares a firm's management hopes to increase the price per share of its stock. This will happen if the P/E ratio of the firm remains the same: as earnings per share increase due to fewer shares outstanding, so too will the price per share (assumed to be the P/E ratio times earnings per share).

When a firm buys back a large number of its own shares, it is in effect saying that it feels its own stock is a better investment then any other available to it at the moment. Crown Cork and Seal has bought back shares ever since John Connelly became President in 1956.

In August 1995, Hershey Foods Company announced it would spend $500,000,000 to repurchase (buyback) 9,000,000 of its common shares of stock, which would then be held as Treasury stock. While Hershey has generated a substantial amount of excess cash from its highly successful chocolate business, it has not been very successful in its efforts to diversify. Thus it considered buying back its own shares to be the best use of its excess cash. Since there will be fewer shares outstanding after the buyback, both Hershey's earnings per share and return on equity will increase. The buyback should also result in a higher price for the remaining shares of Hershey stock. Eastman Kodak, Exxon, IBM, Kellogg and Philip Morris are other examples of large corporations that have repurchased significant numbers of their own shares in recent years.

Acquire Companies with Lower P/E Ratios

By a bit of apparent financial wizardry which will be demonstrated shortly, a firm may increase its earnings per share simply by acquiring another firm which has a lower price/earnings (P/E) ratio than its own. This is true regardless of the business of either of the acquired or the acquiring firm, and subject to only a few assumptions which are normally reasonable to make.

Here is how the process works. Assume Firm A, which has a P/E ratio of 20, acquires Firm B, which has a P/E ratio of 10. Assume further that the stock each firm is traded widely (e.g., on the New York Stock Exchange), and that Firm A's stock sells for $20 per share and Firm B's stock sells for $10 per share. Firm A would therefore give one share of its stock (worth $20) for two shares of stock of Firm B (worth $10 each, or $20 for two shares). Also assume that Firm A has 100 shares outstanding and Firm B has 10 shares outstanding.[10] When the exchange of stock is completed, there will be 105 shares of stock in Firm A outstanding, the ten shares of Firm B's stock having been converted into

---

10.   Small figures have been used for shares outstanding and total shares outstanding to make it easy to follow the arithmetic involved. In practice these figures could be a million or more times larger, but the logic holds regardless of the size of the numbers used.

five shares of Firm A's stock on a two for one basis. This is done under the assumption that the market price of Firm A's stock does not change. This assumption is a good one especially when Firm A is several times larger than Firm B.

The effects of this acquisition are shown in Exhibit 6.3. The earnings of Firm A after the acquisition are the sum of the earnings before the acquisition of Firm A (assume $1.00 per share, or $100 total) and Firm B (assume $1.00 per share, or $10 total), for a total of $110. However, after the acquisition, there are only 105 shares of Firm A's stock outstanding. Hence the earnings per share of Firm A are now $1.05 per share ($110 total earnings divided by 105 shares outstanding) compared to $1.00 per share before the acquisition. The acquisition has resulted in an automatic increase in earnings per share for Firm A of five cents, or five percent.

The result is almost too good to be true. However, as long as there are firms with lower P/E ratios available to be acquired, the process can go on indefinitely. Several conglomerates were quite successful using this "P/E ploy" as their basic strategy during the rising stock market of the 1960's. U.S. Industries acquired over 100 firms without regard to the type of product manufactured or service provided so long as the acquired firm had a lower P/E ratio than did U.S. Industries.

The P/E ploy begins to unravel when the acquiring firm's P/E ratio starts to fall. This can happen even with steadily increasing earnings per share from year to year. Remember, the price per share of common stock is determined by what someone is willing to pay for it at a particular moment, not by whether earnings per share increase each year. This is what happened to U.S. Industries, which spent the 1970s divesting itself of most of the acquisitions it had made in the 1960s.

	Before Acquisition		After Acquisition	
	Firm A	Firm B	Firm A + B	Calculation or Comment
Price per share	$ 20	$ 10	$ 20	Assume no change
Earnings (total)	$ 100	$ 10	$ 110	$100 + $10
Shares outstanding	100	10	105	(100 + 10/2)
Earnings per share	$1.00	$1.00	$1.05	$110 ÷ 105 shares
P/E ratio	20 : 1	10 : 1	19 : 1	$20 ÷ 1.05

Exhibit 6.3. Acquiring a firm with a lower price/earnings ratio. Assume Firm A issues one new share of its stock and exchanges it for two shares of Firm B's stock.

The process can also work in reverse. If in our example Firm A has acquired a firm with a higher P/E ratio, Firm A would have experienced an automatic *decrease* in its earnings per share. One value of a high P/E ratio is that it provides protection against takeovers. The higher the P/E ratio, the more expensive it is to acquire shares of the target firm's stock.

SUMMARY

This completes our discussion of what the general manager should know about earnings per share, book value, and other terminology relating to the financial aspects of a firm. In the next chapter we look at ways to assess the effectiveness of current operation, starting with a discussion of contribution analysis.

Contribution analysis refers to an analysis of the contribution to fixed costs and profit of a business made by each line of business or business segment (i.e., product, product group or division).[1] Contribution to fixed costs and profits (hereafter called contribution to profit) is a useful concept, and is defined as sales minus all directly associated variable costs except taxes. This expression may also be referred to as operating income or pre-tax income. It can be used with respect to the company as a whole or to a product line or business segment of the company. It may also be expressed on a per unit basis: selling price per unit minus all variable costs per unit except taxes.

Contribution analysis is usually done using sales and operating or pre-tax income as the basic input data. The results may be expressed directly in dollar amounts or percentages. While both formats provide useful information, the percentage format permits the general manager to more quickly identify products which are unusually profitable or unprofitable.

Contribution analysis is most frequently applied to diversified firms where it is often instructive to match sales with pre-tax or operating profit by product line or geographic region to obtain contribution to profit.[2] For many years it was not necessary to get data on pre-tax income by product line since most of our large corporations were single product firms with essentially only one line of business. Often the titles reflected the product they made, such as General Motors, Standard Oil, or U.S. Steel. Since World War II large firms have diversified to the point where over 80% of the Fortune 500 industrial firms are now classified as diversified (multi-product) firms, meaning that they have more than one line of business.

By the late 1960s, when the conglomerate movement was at its peak, it was difficult to identify the leading producers in some industries. For example, the major home appliance makers were divisions of major diversified corporations such as General Electric, General Motors and Westinghouse. The Federal Trade Commission (FTC) then started a program whereby publicly owned companies were asked to voluntarily report operating results by segment or line of business, and not just as

---

1. Financial Accounting Standards Board (FASB) Statement Number 14, adopted in 1976, requires a company that does business in more than one industry to report revenue, income and assets data about each significant industry segment. Delineation of a segment requires judgement and should consider the nature of the product and standard product coding systems such as the Standard Industrial Classification (SIC) code. A line of business may consist of either a set of related segments, or a single segment if that segment is large enough. Firms with over 90% of revenues from one line of business report only one line of business. Generally the number of segments reported does not exceed five or six.

2. More specifically, contribution to profit is profit before taxes on income, and the following income and expense items which are not specifically identified with any of the reported segments: equity in earnings of unconsolidated companies, interest expense, corporate administrative and research costs; and other corporate income or expense items. Other terms closely related to contribution to profit are: contribution to fixed cost and profit; earnings before interest and taxes (EBIT); operating profit; pre-tax profit and earnings from operations. Books on accounting and finance and annual reports of corporations often refer to the concept of contribution, but there is wide variation in the terms used to express the concept.

aggregate sales, cost and profit figures.[3] By 1976 FASB Statement Number 14 had made such reporting a requirement. Now that the underlying data is readily available (from an annual report, for example) contribution analysis can provide useful insights into a firm's profitability by products, divisions or geography.

Sometimes such insights will run counter to the initial impression received from a cursory review of a company's annual report. Often such reports contain glamorous color photographs of corporate activities carefully selected to have a favorable impact on the reader regardless of how well or poorly the firm has performed. Nor is the chairman's or president's letter at the front of the annual report much help. I cannot recall ever reading one which was pessimistic about the firm's future no matter how precarious its current financial condition.

HOW TO DO IT

Contribution analysis can be carried out either in dollar amounts or in percentages. The two ways of representing the same data are best shown through an example. In Exhibit 7.1, the XYZ Company is assumed to have annual sales of $150,000,000 and annual pre-tax income of $10,000,000 spread as shown over three product lines. The figures in Exhibit 7.1 are in dollar amounts. Often it is more useful for purposes of analysis to have them expressed in percentages as in Exhibit 7.2. Similar data should be prepared for several years to facilitate indentifying trends.

Contribution analysis is a good tool for the general manager to use to see if management's written analysis of operations is supported by the facts. Toward this end it is helpful to ask three questions:

1. *Where does the firm make most of its money?*

Knowing nothing about a particular firm, it is reasonable to assume that each product should have the same relative degree of profitability, meaning that a product's pre-tax income should be proportional to its sales. Thus if a particular product line or segment of the XYZ Company accounts for 30% of sales, we start by assuming that it should also contribute 30% (approximately) to its pre-tax income. However, profitability and sales are rarely so nicely balanced. Many time contribution analysis will show that a disproportionate amount of a firm's pre-tax income comes from only one or two products or geographic areas.

2. *What trends in profitability are discernible?*

A review of the pre-tax income figures for a period of years (five years should be adequate) will

---

3. For a discussion of the Federal Trade Commission program, see B.J. Linder and Allan H. Savage, "The Line of Business Program—The FTC's New Tool," *California Management Review*, Summer 1979, pp. 57-69.

quickly reveal which products are improving, which are staying the same, which are declining, and which are cyclical in nature.

3. Which products may be divested in the next few years?

Products which lose money for a period of years or which don't perform up to profit expectations are prime candidates for managerial attention, either to turn them around or to divest them. Often an alert analyst can detect major problem areas in a company before top management makes them known publicly.

	(Millions of Dollars)											
	Product A		**Product B**		**Product C**		**Totals**	
Year	Sales	Pre-tax Income	Sales	Pre-tax Income	Sales	Pre-tax Income	Sales	Pre-tax Income
19XX	$75	$3	$50	$5	$25	$2	$150	$10

Exhibit 7.1. Sales and pre-tax income by product line, XYZ Company (in dollars).

	(Expressed in Percent)											
	Product A		**Product B**		**Product C**		**Totals**	
Year	Sales	Pre-tax Income	Sales	Pre-tax Income	Sales	Pre-tax Income	Sales	Pre-tax Income
19XX	50%	30%	33.3%	50%	16.7%	20%	100%	100%

Exhibit 7.2. Sales and pre-tax income by product line, XYZ Company (in percent).

Gillette: An Example of Product Line Contribution Analysis

The Gillette Company is an excellent example of the usefulness of contribution analysis in answering the three questions posed above. Gillette is one of the best known consumer product brand names in the United States. King Gillette invented the razor with a disposable blade in 1895 and the company he founded still dominates the shaving market. In recent years Gillette, like many other companies, has diversified into other consumer product areas as well. Exhibit 7.3 shows the percent of sales and pre-tax income for each of Gillette's five product lines (segments).

Now to answer the three basic questions.

1. Where does Gillette make its money?

The answer is clear from a cursory examination of Exhibit 7.3. In 1993 70% of Gillette's pre-tax profit came from Blades & Razors, which in turn represented only 39% of Gillette's total sales. Toiletries and Cosmetics contributed only 5% of pre-tax income, although they accounted for 19% of sales. Clearly Toiletries and Cosmetics are far less profitable than blades and razors. The same is true for the other three major product areas, Stationary Products, Braun Products and Oral-B Products. The data indicate that despite efforts to diversify, Gillette was still a one product company as of 1993, getting the bulk of its profits from the sales of razors and blades.

Year	Blades & Razors		Toiletries & Cosmetics		Stationary Products		Braun Products		Oral-B Products	
	Sales	Pre-tax	Sales	Pre-tax	Sales	Pre-tax	Sales	Pre-tax	Sales	Pre-tax
1993	39%	70%	19%	5%	12%	6%	23%	15%	7%	4%
1992	38	66	19	9	10	5	26	16	7	4
1991	37	62	20	13	10	5	26	16	7	4
1990	36	60	22	13	11	8	25	15	6	4
1989	32	62	27	10	11	10	24	15	6	3

Exhibit 7.3. Contribution analysis of Gillette Company, in percent. Adapted from 1993 Gillette Company *Annual Report*, p. 39.

2. *What profitability trends are discernible?*

Pre-tax profit attributable to Blades & Razors has risen from 62% in 1989 to 70% in 1993. Meanwhile, the pre-tax income attributable to both Toiletries & Cosmetics and to Stationary Products has fallen significantly. Braun Products and Oral-B Products have remained constant. The most profitable product line by far is Blades & Razors. By 1993, 70% of Gillette's pre-tax profit came on the 39% of sales attributed to Blades & Razors.

3. *What products are candidates for divestiture?*

Toiletries & Cosmetics and Stationary Products each appear to be candidates for divestiture. Together, they accounted for 31% of sales in 1993, but only 11% of pre-tax profit. Since Toiletries & Cosmetics are so closely related to Blades & Razors, Gillette is less likely to divest that division than it is Stationary Products, which includes writing instruments. Unless sales of Oral-B Products can be increased, that division may also be a candidate for divestiture. It should come as no surprise that Gillette's annual reports over the years have discussed the possibility of divesting itself of one or more of these divisions.

As the Gillette example shows, contribution analysis can quickly bring to light information that is not often apparent from a casual review of an annual report or simply by reading the Chairman's letter to shareholders.

Coca-Cola : An Example of Geographic Contribution Analysis

Coca-Cola is the world's largest soft drink company, with sales in 1994 of $16.1 billion, pre-tax profit of $3.7 billion, and net income of $2.6 billion. In Exhibit 7.4, a contribution analysis is presented on Coca-Cola's sales grouped into four geographic regions.

Year	United States		Europe		Pacific & Canada		Africa & Latin America	
	Sales	Pre-tax	Sales	Pre-tax	Sales	Pre-tax	Sales	Pre-tax
1994	32%	21%	31%	29%	22%	29%	15%	21%
1993	33	22	32	29	21	29	14	20
1992	33	21	35	31	19	28	13	20

Exhibit 7.4. Contribution Analysis of Coca-Cola Company, in percent. Adapted from 1994 Coca-Cola *Annual Report*, p. 65.

The following conclusions can be drawn from Exhibit 7.4.

1. Coca-Cola is truly an international company. It gets 68% of its sales and 79% of its pre-tax profits from operations outside the United States.
2. European and U.S. sales are about equal, but Europe contributes about 50% more in pre-tax profits.
3. Europe and the U.S. comprise about two-thirds of Coca-Cola's sales, but they only contribute about half its pre-tax profits.
4. The greatest growth opportunities lie in the rest of the world, where both sales and pre-tax profits as a percent of total sales and pre-tax profits are increasing.

On the basis of this analysis, it is no surprise to find the following statement about worldwide availability of its products in the 1994 Coca-Cola Annual Report (p. 10):

The number of consumers we can actively reach out to with our products climbed from less than 2.2 billion in 1984 to more than 5.2 billion in 1994. The number of countries in which we are actively conducting business totaled more than 195 in 1994, while the number of nations in which we do not do business dwindled to fewer than 20.

Campbell Soup: Another Example of Geographic Contribution Analysis

Campbell Soup Company is the world's largest maker of canned soups. It also markets a variety of other food products worldwide, such as bakery products, pickles and canned juices. Campbell had 1994 sales of $6.7 billion , pre-tax profit of $1.1 billion, and net income of $630 million. In his letter to shareholders in the 1994 Annual Report, CEO David Johnson writes,

...Campbell Soup Company is engaged in a global consumer crusade. It springs from our vision of

Campbell Brands Preferred Around the World. The aim is to convert millions of new customers to Campbell brands every year.

That may be his goal, but the geographical contribution analysis in Exhibit 7.5 indicates that progress thus far is slow.

Year	United States		Europe		Pacific & Canada	
	Sales	Pre-tax	Sales	Pre-tax	Sales	Pre-tax
1994	59%	73%	18%	14%	23%	13%
1993	61	94	15	16	24	(10)
1992	63	80	15	10	24	10

Exhibit 7.5. Contribution Analysis of Campbell Soup Company in percent. Adapted from 1994 Campbell Soup Company *Annual Report*, p. 21.

Exhibit 7.5 shows that a disproportionate amount of sales (about 60%) and pre-tax profits (about 75%) still come from the United States. Unlike Coca-Cola, which gets most of its profits from abroad, Campbell gets little more than twenty percent of its profit from overseas sales. Further, the percent of international sales isn't rising. Used in this way, contribution analysis can bring a touch of realism to the CEO's comments in a firm's annual report. It can also highlight a major challenge facing management, such as international expansion in the case of Campbell Soup Company.

SOURCES OF LINE OF BUSINESS OR SEGMENT DATA

The three primary sources of data on profitability by line of business or segment for publicly held firms are:

1. The firm's annual report (segment information is often included at the end of the financial section).
2. The *Value Line Investment Survey* data sheet on the firm.
3. *Moody's* or *Standard and Poor's Corporate Records*.

One or more of these is usually available either in school of business libraries or in the reference area of most public libraries.

SUMMARY

Contribution analysis is an invaluable way to find out where a company with more than one significant product line or business gets most of its sales and makes most of its money. A contribution analysis can also be done by geographic region to show which regions contribute most to a company's sales and pre-tax profits. Whenever the data is available, a contribution analysis should be done in conjunction with free cash flow analysis and ratio analysis, discussed in chapters 2 and 3 respectively. Done as a package, free cash flow analysis, ratio analysis and contribution analysis will reveal much about the profitability of a firm with two or more business segments.

Break-even analysis emphasizes the relationship between revenue and various cost factors and how they affect profitability.[1] The *break-even point* is defined as the point at which sales or revenues for a product or business equal the sum of all costs (fixed and variable) associated with that product or business. The product or business will be profitable above this level of sales and unprofitable below it.

The basic break-even relationship is expressed as follows:

$$(8–1) \text{ Sales (break-even)} = \frac{\text{Fixed costs}}{1 - \dfrac{\text{Variable cost per unit}}{\text{Selling price per unit}}}$$

Thus if a firm's fixed costs are $10,000,000 per year, variable cost per unit sold is $800 and selling price is $1,000 per unit, break-even will occur when sales reach $50,000,000. Another way to look at this situation is to note that of each dollar of sales, twenty cents are left over after paying the variable costs of eighty cents. (This is based on the observation that variable costs are eighty percent of sales.) Then twenty cents per dollar of sales times sales at break-even ($50,000,000) equals fixed costs of $10,000,000.

The lower the break-even point, the better. Note that the break-even point can be lowered by:

- reducing fixed costs
- reducing variable costs; or
- increasing selling price.

When Lee Iacocca became chairman of Chrysler Corporation in 1978, he found that even at full production Chrysler was operating several billion dollars *below* its break-even point. His program of restoring Chrysler to profitability consisted of changing all three key variables in break-even analysis. He quickly reduced fixed costs by reducing excess corporate staff, reduced variable costs per car by asking for wage concessions from the union, and increased sales by raising selling price per car by two percent.

---

1. Break-even analysis differs from contribution analysis, the topic of Chapter 7, in that contribution analysis is based on historical data while break-even analysis is oriented toward estimating results for a future period of time.

FIXED AND VARIABLE COSTS

For purposes of break-even analysis, costs are divided into fixed costs and variable costs:

1. *Fixed costs.* These are *indirect costs* associated with being in business. They can be visualized as the costs that would accrue even if no units were produced during the year. (By analogy, you might think of the costs that would accrue if you owned a house but did not live in it, or owned a car but did not drive it.) Fixed business costs generally include rent, interest charges, property taxes (but not income taxes), insurance, executive salaries, advertising allocations and allowance for depreciation of plant and equipment.[2] At first it might appear that the initial, one time cost of building the plant has been taken into account. However, the yearly charges for depreciation for plant and equipment include a portion of the initial construction cost. Hence the cost of building the plant has in fact been accounted for.

2. *Variable costs.* Variable costs are costs that can be associated *directly* with the production of a particular product or performance of a specific service. For a manufacturing or industrial business these include direct materials, direct labor, packaging, fuel, supplies, and sales commissions. Variable costs represent the direct charges associated with making a unit of the final product. For purposes of break-even analysis, these are generally assumed to be constant or fixed per unit regardless of the level of output. This means that variable costs increase directly with production (e.g., if output doubles, then variable costs also double). For a retail business, variable costs can be considered to consist entirely of merchandise for resale.

CONTRIBUTION TO PROFIT

Once variable cost per unit is known and a selling price per unit has been set, contribution to profit per unit sold can be found as follows:

$$(8\text{-}3) \quad \begin{matrix} \text{Contribution} \\ \text{to profit per} \\ \text{dollar of sales} \end{matrix} = \begin{matrix} \text{Selling price} \\ \text{per unit} \end{matrix} - \begin{matrix} \text{Variable cost} \\ \text{per unit} \end{matrix}$$

If several products are involved, a weighted average may be used for selling price per unit and variable cost per unit to simply the analysis.

It may be easier to find contribution to profit per dollar of sales rather than per unit sold. Contribution to profit per dollar of sales is found by dividing both sides of the equation (8-3) by selling price per unit:

---

2. As volume increases fixed cost per unit decreases until some upper limit is reached, such as the plant operating at full capacity. Profitability increases when fixed cost per unit decreases. This helps explain the desire of many large firms to mass produce a standardized item, such as automobiles or computers, or to have many retail stores, where the overhead can be spread over as many units as possible.

$$(8\text{-}4) \begin{array}{l} \text{Contribution} \\ \text{to profit per} \\ \text{dollar of sales} \end{array} = 1 - \frac{\text{Variable cost per unit}}{\text{Selling price per unit}}$$

Sometimes contribution to profit per dollar of sales can be estimated directly, as in a retail business. If the only variable costs are the purchase of goods for resale, which on average cost 70 percent of retail sales value (a markup of 30/70 or 42.8%), then the average contribution to profit per dollar of sales is thirty cents.

BREAK-EVEN EQUATIONS

Thus far we have talked in general terms about break-even analysis. Now we are ready for the equations which will facilitate calculations associated with break-even analysis. The variables commonly used are defined below. (Variables starting with a capital letter refer to *Total* amounts and variables starting with small letters refer to *per unit* amounts.)

TR = total revenue in dollars

TFC = total cost in dollars

VC = total variable costs

FC = total fixed costs

vc = variable cost per unit in dollars

sp = selling price per unit in dollars

BEP = break-even point (expressed in dollars of sales, units sold, percent of capacity, or other units, as appropriate.)

The equations are as follows for calculating the break-even point for sales as a function of three alternatives measures of output: dollars of sales, units sold, or percent of capacity utilized:

$$(8\text{-}6) \text{ BEP (\$ of sales)} = \frac{\text{TFC}}{1 - \text{vc/sp}}$$

$$(8\text{-}7) \text{ BEP (units sold)} = \frac{\text{TFC}}{\text{sp} - \text{vc}}$$

[Obtained by dividing (8-6) by sp (price per unit)]

$$(8\text{-}8) \text{ BEP (\% of capacity)} = \frac{\text{TFC} \times 100\%}{(\text{sp} - \text{vc}) \text{ (Facility capacity in units)}}$$

[Obtained by dividing (8-7) by facility capacity in units and multiplying by 100 to convert to percent.]

While the equations just given can be used to calculate the break-even point directly, it is often instructive to draw a chart which depicts the break-even analysis. The break-even chart shows the relationship between total revenue (sales) and total costs (the sum of fixed costs and variable costs) at different levels of output. As with equations (8-6), (8-7) and (8-8), output may be expressed in dollars of sales, units sold or percent of capacity utilized.

GRAPHICAL REPRESENTATION OF BREAK-EVEN ANALYSIS

Break-even charts are drawn with the vertical (y) axis representing costs in dollars as a function of output, which is expressed along the horizontal (x) axis. The simplest measure of output is dollar volume of sales. The profit (or loss) for any level of sales is the difference between that level of sales and costs for that level of sales.

The basic break-even chart is drawn as follows:

1. *Draw the total revenue line.*This is a straight line rising at a 45° angle from the origin. (This line represents the situation where there are no fixed costs and variable costs are always exactly equal to sales. In practice, such a situation is extremely unlikely to occur.)

2. *Draw the total fixed cost line.* Find the point on the vertical (y) axis that corresponds to fixed costs, then draw a horizontal line. (This indicates that fixed costs do not change as sales [as measured along the x axis] change. In fact, this is why fixed costs are called fixed costs.)

3. *Draw the variable cost line.* Variable costs increase in direct proportion to sales. If a certain item has a variable cost of $10 associated with it, the variable cost for two items will be $20 (2 × $10). This line is drawn *on top* of the total fixed cost line just drawn in step 2. This is because at any level of output fixed costs and variable costs are *additive*, and the sum of these two lines gives the total cost line, which is what we really want. (Two points are necessary to draw this line. One of them is always the point where the fixed cost line crosses the vertical (y) axis. The other can be found by moving along the x axis to a convenient level of sales, then moving directly upward by the amount of variable costs associated with this level of sales. This is the second point. Connect these points by a straight line to get the desired total cost line.)

4. *Locate the break-even point.* This is the amount of sales corresponding to the intersection of the total cost line and the 45° angle line representing sales.

Exhibit 8.1 demonstrates a basic break-even situation where the measure of output is sales expressed in thousands of dollars. In this example, selling price per unit (sp) is $1,000, variable cost per unit (vc) is $500, fixed costs are $20,000 and facility capacity is 80 units. The break-even level of sales is $40,000.

The x axis can be transformed to express sales in other formats, such as units sold or percent of facility capacity:

$$\text{x-axis point in units sold} \quad = \quad \frac{\text{x-axis point in dollars of sales}}{\text{Selling price per unit}}$$

$$\begin{array}{c}\text{x-axis point in percent of} \\ \text{facility capacity}\end{array} \quad = \quad \frac{\text{x-axis point in units sold} \times 100}{\text{Facility capacity in units}}$$

Exhibit 8.2 uses two alternative measures of output along the x-axis: units sold and percent of capacity.

Other measures of output may be more appropriate in certain situations. For a retail store sales per square foot would be a more meaningful measure of output than percent of facility capacity. In this case it would also be useful for purposes of comparison to indicate the industry standard for the measure of output chosen along the x-axis. Thus if the national average is sales of $200 per square foot for a particular type of retail store, so indicate on the x-axis to show how the store under consideration compares.

INFORMATION CONTAINED IN BREAK-EVEN ANALYSIS

The perceptive general manager can learn a great deal from a well prepared break-even analysis, starting with the shape of the break-even chart itself. Representative cases are discussed in Exhibit 8-3. Note that contribution to profit per dollar of sales in Exhibit 8.3 could also be read as contribution as a percent of sales. Thus a contribution to profit of ten cents per dollar of sales is the same as a contribution to profit of ten percent on sales. After working with break-even analysis for a period of time, a general manger appreciates the desirability of a high contribution of profit per dollar of sales (slope of variable cost line much less than one) and low fixed costs. On the other hand, the undesirability of a business with a low contribution to profit per dollar of sales (slope of variable cost line nearly equal to one) and high fixed costs should also be apparent.

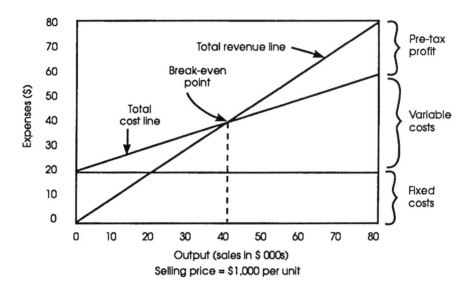

Exhibit 8.1. Break-even chart where measure of output is dollars of sales.

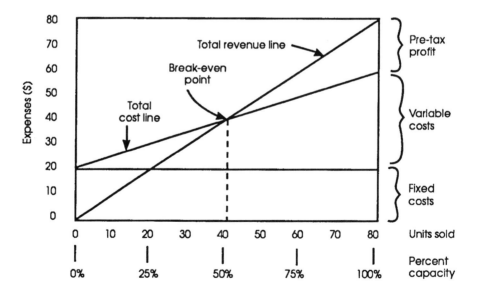

Exhibit 8.2. Break-even chart where measures of output are units sold and percent of capacity.

Situation	Contribution to Profit per Dollar of Sales	Fixed Costs	Comments
1.	≤ 0	Doesn't matter	Disaster. Can never make a profit, no matter how many units are sold, since variable cost is greater than selling price per unit.
2.	Low 1–10 cents	Moderate to high	Almost as bad. Large volume needed to cover fixed costs. Typical of retailing firms.
3.	Low 1–10 cents	Low	Need high volume to attain reasonable profit.
4.	Normal 20–40 cents	Moderate to high	Can attain reasonable profits on reasonable volume; typical of single plant or store.
5.	Normal 20–40 cents	Low	High profits available on reasonable sales. Typical of a mail order business or a manufacturer's agent.
6.	High 40–60 cents	Moderate to high	High volume will yield high profits, as with bulk chemical producers or IBM's sales of mainframe computing systems.
7.	Very high > 60 cents	Low	Best of all worlds! Probably a monopoly or protected by patents, like Polaroid or Xerox in their early years.

Exhibit 8.3. Break-even situations.

USING BREAK-EVEN ANALYSIS IN PRESENTATIONS

When a new venture or product is being introduced, those responsible for approving it often request that a presentation be made to them. A well prepared break-even chart can be an invaluable part of such a presentation. However, care must be taken to select an appropriate measure of output, or else the break-even analysis may lose much of its impact.

Reviewers attempt to visualize results in simple terms meaningful to them as the presentation is being made. For example, when flying on an airplane or eating in a restaurant, a person can glance at the number of seats that are filled and say, "The place is jammed; they must be making money hand over fist." In economic terms this means they are operating well above the break-even point. On the other hand, a plane or restaurant that is almost empty is probably operating well below break-even and might elicit a comment to the effect "They must be losing their shirts here." In these familiar examples an easily understandable measure is the percentage of seats that need to be filled on the average for the business to break-even.

Some examples of good and poor measures of break-even are given in Exhibit 8.4. Good measures are usually expressed as a ratio (e.g., percentage of capacity) while poor measures are usually expressed as an absolute number (e.g., units produced).

Situation	Measure of Output	
	Good	Poor
Airline route	% of seats filled per plane per flight	Flights per year
Plant/factory	% of capacity	Units produced
Indoor tennis club	% of available court hours that must be used each day, week or month	Number of club members
Retail store	Sales per squre foot (compare to national average)	Total units sold

Exhibit 8.4. Examples of good and poor measures of output.

SHORTCOMINGS OF BREAK-EVEN ANALYSIS

Break-even analysis provides some very useful insights into the operation and profitability of a business. However, break-even analysis is usually a fairly simplified representation of reality. Here are some considerations that should be kept in mind when performing (or reviewing) a break-even analysis:

1. *Selling price.* While this is perhaps the most important variable in the whole analysis, few managers can be certain that external factors (e.g., a sluggish economy, competitors' actions) won't adversely affect sales at the price assumed. A lower selling price will increase the break-even point. In an extreme case it may push it beyond the firm's production capacity.
2. *Costs.* The firm needs a good cost accounting system which takes into account such factors as increases or decreases in inventory levels during the period in question. This is particularly difficult when an entirely new product or venture is planned.
3. *Assumed linear relationships.* Break-even analysis as presented here assumes that variable costs always bear a linear relationship to sales. This is not always a good assumption. For example, due to the "learning curve" phenomenon where we tend to do a task better (faster or at lower cost) when we do it more often, variable cost per unit, particularly labor cost, may actually decrease as volume of output increases.[3] Also, plant or facility capacity will be reached at some point. And with new plant and equipment come additional fixed costs which may raise the break-even point.
4. *Fixed or variable costs.* Costs that are fixed in the short run may well be variable in the long run, such as wage rates or the productivity of equipment. Some costs may be partly variable and partly fixed. Consider a retail store where labor may technically be a variable cost since it varies

---

3. See, for example, Winfred B. Hirchman, "Profit From the Learning Curve," *Harvard Business Review*, January-February 1964, pp. 125-129.

with volume (more staff is needed at peak periods, such as holidays). However, total labor costs may be fairly steady from year to year, and hence can be considered fixed of purposes of analysis.

Exhibit 8.5 shows how the basic break-even chart can be drawn so that it includes the major segments of cost and how they change with increased output for a typical small manufacturing firm. Note how much information of use to the general manager is contained in this break-even chart:

1. Break-even occurs at 62.5% of plant capacity and a sales volume of $14,000,000.
2. New facilities (or additional shift) will be needed if sales volume exceeds $22,000,000, which is the sales volume when the plant is operating at 100% capacity for one shift.
3. Profits can be increased by increasing selling price, but this may be hard to do and still maintain desired volume.
4. Profits can be increased by reducing costs. Direct materials are the largest component of variable cost in Exhibit 8.5 and should be looked at closely.

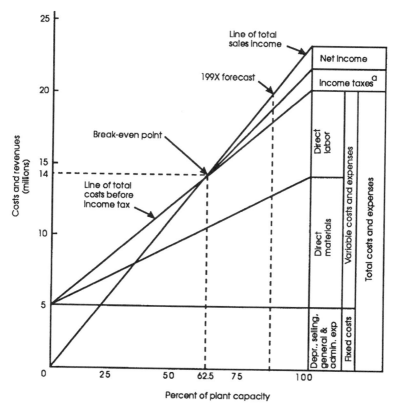

Exhibit 8.5. Break-even chart for XYZ Company showing major segments of cost.

Note that income taxes are only taken into account *above* the break-even point. Below the break-even point the company is operating at a loss and will have no income taxes. Should the company have several plants, and a break-even chart for each one, then taxes would be taken into account on the *total* pre-tax net income of all the plants.

SUMMARY

Break-even analysis is a very useful analytical tool. Used properly, it can give the general manager much insight not only into current operation but also into what effect changes in pricing, volume and costs can have on profitability. It is an excellent way to express the three key variables of sales, fixed cost and variable cost in a format that is informative, concise and easy to understand when properly presented.

PAYBACK PERIOD AND DISCOUNTED CASH FLOW

When considering an investment in new plant or equipment (or both), the general manager will often want to know how long it will take for the investment to pay for itself. This period of time is called the *payback period*. The payback period is closely related to the discussion of break-even analysis in Chapter 8. The break-even point, usually expressed as a measure of output (sales, units sold or percent of capacity), referred to the point in time *during a period* of operations (e.g., a year) where revenues equalled the total of fixed and variable costs (including depreciation). The payback period is the *length of time* until the accumulated cash flow (net income plus depreciation) equals the amount of an initial investment.[1]

An example of determining the payback period for an investment is given in Exhibit 9.1. The calculations are in dollars and are not adjusted for the time value of money. In this example it will take three years to recover the initial investment and the payback period is thus three years. Column (b) in Exhibit 9.1 is labeled cash flow because it represents the actual dollars that flow in (or out) during the life of the investment. (Remember that cash flow includes depreciation charges for the period.)

General mangers like to use payback period as one way to evaluate a potential investment for the following reasons:

1. The calculations are easy to do; they only involve addition and subtraction once the cash inflows and outflows have been estimated.
2. The concepts are easily understood by managers who may have little background in finance.
3. The estimate of cash inflows and outflows for each period (year, quarter) quickly shows whether it will be necessary to borrow money during the project, and if so, about how much.
4. The effects of different levels of sales on the payback period can be readily determined.
5. A limit on the payback period may be specified at the start of the analysis. For example, a firm may decide that all investments in new plant and equipment must have a payback period of two years or less. (Such short payback requirements are not uncommon in industry; I remember hearing a vice-president of a Fortune 500 company say that his firm required all projects to pay for themselves in six months or less!)

---

1. Sometimes payback is calculated by determining the length of time until net income equals the cost of the investment. This will overstate the payback period if depreciation is involved (and it almost always is), since depreciation is a non-cash charge against earnings, and must be added to net income to get cash flow.

However, there are also shortcomings to using payback period as the primary criterion for accepting or rejecting an investment alternative.

1. Payback period does not provide a very reliable indication on long term projects where the time value of money can have a much greater impact than it does on short term projects.
2. There is no mechanism to indicate preference for a project where the cash inflows are highest in the early years of the project. For example, we would all prefer a project with returns of $8,000, $1,000 and $1,000 to one which returned $1,000, $1,000 and $8,000 over the same three year period, even though the total inflows ($10,000) are the same. If the payback period is greater than three years, the payback criterion alone does not indicate which set of cash flows would be more desirable.

Year	Expenditures for Investment (a)	Estimated Cash Flow from Investment (b)	Cumulative Total (a) + (b)
0	24,000	---	−24,000
1	---	8,000	−16,000
2	---	8,000	−8,000
3	---	8,000	0
4	---	8,000	+8,000
5	---	8,000	+16,000

Exhibit 9.1. Payback period example.

For these reasons, most books on finance spend little time discussing payback period as a way to evaluate proposed investments. Instead, they concentrate on the use of discounted cash flow techniques which take the time value of money explicitly into account when evaluating investment alternatives.

DISCOUNTED CASH FLOW METHODS

Two discounted cash flow methods are in general use, one based on calculating the *net present value* of a potential investment, the other its *internal rate of return*. We will review the basic principles of each of these approaches, but first we need to review how to calculate the present value of a dollar received at a future date.

A dollar received today is worth more than a dollar received a year from now because it can earn a rate of return (e.g., interest) during the year. The present value of a dollar to be received at a future date (called its present value) can be found by discounting its value at the future date back to the present. The appropriate discount factor is the earnings rate expected on the dollar for the interim. If taxes are pertinent, they should be subtracted from the annual cash flows before the discounted cash flow analysis is performed.

The general expression for the present value of a sum of money received at a future time is:

$$(9\text{-}1)\ \text{NPV} = \frac{S}{(1+i)^n}$$

where

S = sum of money received

i = earnings rate for each period

n = number of periods

For example, the present value of $1 received three years from now with an earnings rate of 10% would be:

$$\text{NPV} = \frac{1}{(1+.1)^3} = .751$$

The general expression for the present value of a set of payments made or received periodically is:

$$(9\text{-}2)\ \text{NPV} = \frac{S}{(1+i)^1} + \frac{S}{(1+i)^2} + \ldots + \frac{S}{(1+i)^n} =$$

$$\sum_{j=1}^{n} \frac{S}{(1+i)^j} = S \sum_{j=1}^{n} \frac{1}{(1+i)^j}$$

where

S = sum of money received in each period

i = earnings rate for each period

j = index of period (j = 1,2,3, . . ., n)

n = number of periods

For example, the present value of $1 received for each of the next three years with an earnings rate of 10% would be:

$$\text{NPV} = \frac{\$1}{(1+.1)^1} + \frac{\$1}{(1+.1)^2} + \frac{\$1}{(1+.1)^3} = \$2.487$$

It is rarely necessary to do all the arithmetic, as tables of present values are readily available and the discounting factor can be looked up directly. Appendix C is a table of the present value of a dollar for a wide range of years. It can be used to check the result just given. Many pocket calculators also have present value function keys on them which will quickly perform the calculations.

THE NET PRESENT VALUE METHOD

In the net present value method of evaluating a proposed investment, the time value of money is explicitly taken into account when evaluating all cash inflows and outflows. This approach is shown graphically in Exhibit 9.2, where the arrows represent the magnitude and direction (positive or negative) of the cash flows in each period for the life of the project.

This relationship can also be expressed in the form of an equation as follows:

$$NPV = \frac{CF_1}{(1+i)^1} + \frac{CF_2}{(1+i)^2} + \ldots + \frac{CF_n}{(1+i)^n}$$

or

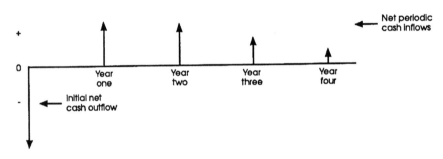

Exhibit 9.2. Representation of cash flows over time.

$$(9\text{-}3)\ NPV = \sum_{j=1}^{n} \frac{CF_j}{(1+i)^j}$$

where

NPV = Net present value of cash inflows for n periods

CF_j = cash flow in period j

j = index or period (j = 1,2,3, . . ., n)

n = number of periods

i = earnings rate for each period (rate of return)

In equations (9-3) the earnings rate i is usually assumed to be the same for each period. The most common period is one year, but other periods could be used as long as the earnings rate is adjusted accordingly.

The simplest decision rule for accepting the project is whether the Net Present Value (NPV) computed in equation (9-3) is greater than the amount of the initial investment I. If it is, accept the project; if it isn't, reject the project.

Computing NPV in equation (9-3) is greatly simplified when the cash flows (the CF_j values) are the same in each period. Then equation (9-3) can be written as follows:

$$(9\text{-}4)\ NPV\ =\ CF \sum_{j=1}^{n} \frac{1}{(1+i)^j}$$

As an application of this technique let us reconsider the payback problem considered in Exhibit 9.1. Assuming a 15% return for each year, present value factors are applied to the cash flows for each year as shown in Exhibit 9.3. A comparison of Exhibit 9-3 with Exhibit 9-1 shows that the discounted cash flow method simply gives an *appropriate weight* (i.e., the present value factors in column (c)) to each year's cash flow. Remember that in the payback period method we made no attempt to take the time value of money into account in each year's cash flow.

The same result can be obtained by applying equation (9-4) since the cash inflows (CF) are equal in years one through five. With i = .15, the value of a dollar received each year for five years can be found directly from Appendix D to be 3.352.

Year	Expenditures for investment (a)	Estimated Cash Flow from Investment (b)	Present Value Factor[a] (c)	Present Value of Cash Flow (d)	Cumulative Net Present Value of Cash Flow (e)
0	24,000	---	1	−24,000	−24,000
1	---	8,000	.870	6,960	−17,040
2	---	8,000	.756	6,048	−10,992
3	---	8,000	.658	5,264	−5,728
4	---	8,000	.572	4,576	−1,152
5	---	8,000	.497	3,976	+2.824

[a]From Appendix C using rate of return of 15%

Exhibit 9.3. Payback period example using net present values.

$$NPV = CF \sum_{j=1}^{n} \frac{1}{(1+i)^j}$$

$$= \$8,000 \times \sum_{j=1}^{n} \frac{1}{(1+.15)^j}$$

$$= \$8,000 \times 3.352 = \$26,816$$

The difference between NPV and I (the investment) is $2,816 ($26,816 – $24,000) which is the same (except for rounding) as the $2,824 obtained with the step by step procedure used in Exhibit 9.3.

In this case the results are changed considerably: break-even isn't achieved until several months into the fifth year rather than at the end of year three. The results would be even more dramatic if the earnings rate i for each period was larger. For example, if i = .25, Appendix D shows the value of a dollar received each year for five years would be 2.689. The net present value of the cash inflows would then be $2.689 \times \$8,000$ or $21,512. Since this is $2,488 *less* than the initial investment of $24,000, the project would be rejected according to the net present value criterion.

THE INTERNAL RATE OF RETURN METHOD

The internal rate of return (IRR) method is similar to the net present value method, except that I (for investment) is written in place of NPV in equation (9-3):

$$(9\text{-}5) \quad I = \sum_{j=1}^{n} \frac{CF_j}{(1+i)^j}$$

Now equation (9-5) is solved for i, which is called the internal rate of return (IRR). If the CF_j's are equal, equation (9-5) can be rewritten as follows and is not too difficult to solve by trying various values of i with the aid of Appendix D or a pocket calculator.

$$I = CF \sum_{j=1}^{n} \frac{1}{(1+i)^j}$$

If the CF_j's are not equal and n is greater than two, then use of a specialized computer program will probably be necessary to get a good solution.[2]

_____

2. Remember that there are as many solutions to an equation as the highest order power present in it. A quadratic equation (an equation with squared terms in it) has two solutions, a cubic equation three, and so on. One or more of these solutions may be "impossible" (e.g., a negative value) given the problem you are solving. Always make sure the results make sense in light of the problem being solved.

Returning to our example we solve for i as follows:

$$I = CF \sum_{j=1}^{n} \frac{1}{(1+i)^j}$$

$$24,000 = 8,000 \sum_{j=1}^{5} \frac{1}{(1+i)^j}$$

$$\text{or} \sum_{j=1}^{5} \frac{1}{(1+i)^j} = 3$$

From Appendix D, we find that for i = 20%, the value of the expression is 2.991. Thus i (the internal rate of return) is just a bit above 20%.

The internal rate of return is frequently used as a decision rule for accepting or rejecting projects. For example, the XYZ Company may only accept projects that have an internal rate of return of 20% or greater.

Discounted cash flow techniques offer a more sophisticated method of analysis than calculation of the payback period. All general managers whose jobs require them to deal to any great extent with financial matters that extend over a period of years, such as capital budgeting, should be familiar with them. However, these methods also have limitations:

1. Results may vary widely depending on the assumptions made about the cost of money and the rate of return to be earned on investments in future years.[3]
2. It takes enough more effort (even with the help of a pocket calculator) to do the calculations associated with a discounted cash flow analysis to make many managers instinctively prefer the simpler arithmetic involved with computing the payback period.
3. Non-quantitative factors such as desire to develop a new product, select only projects above a certain size, or fill out an existing product line may be given greater emphasis when selecting investments than the results of the cash flow analysis. This is good, because common sense should always be used as well as financial criteria when selecting which investment alternatives to fund.

---

3. While the net present value and internal rate of return methods generally lead to the same decision on whether or not to accept a proposed investment, they do not always do so. This is because the internal rate of return method all cash flows are assumed to be reinvested at the internal rate of return. This may not be realistic, especially if the internal rate of return is very high (above 25%). The net present value method assumes all cash inflows are reinvested at the rate of return used in evaluating the proposed investment.

SUMMARY

The arguments for using discounted cash flow techniques to evaluate investment alternatives have considerable merit, particularly for the financial specialist. Yet for the general manager who wants a *reasonably accurate* evaluation that can be prepared quickly, the payback period without regard to the time value of money is often perfectly adequate. This is particularly true for investments of short duration (two years or less) where, due to the short period of time involved, all methods will give about the same result. However, when the time period of the proposed investment is long and the outcome fairly predictable (as in the five to ten years required to bring a new pharmaceutical product to market) discounted cash flow techniques are a much sounder way to evaluate investment alternatives.

Two post-World War II events have made exchange rates a topic of importance to general managers. One is the great increase in international trade, both in finished goods and raw materials. The other is the 1971 agreement by Western nations to abandon fixed exchange rates and let currencies fluctuate with respect to each other. Regardless of cause, fluctuations in exchange rates can have a significant impact on a firm's financial performance.

INTERNATIONAL MONETARY SYSTEMS

Currencies of nations can either be *fixed* to a common point of reference (usually gold) or they can *float*, meaning they have no fixed point of reference. At the Bretton Woods, New Hampshire, conference in 1944 toward the end of World War II, the Western nations agreed to go on the gold standard. In brief, this meant that:

- nations defined their currencies in grains of gold, payable on demand to both private citizens and central banks.
- rates of exchange between different currencies were linked, giving the Western world what amounted to a single international medium of exchange.
- nations losing gold because of balance of trade difficulties were expected to tighten credit (increase interest rates) at home to attract investment of foreign currencies (a return of gold), while those gaining gold were expected to do the opposite.

In short, the gold standard meant that the currencies of Western nations could be converted into gold at a fixed rate. Thus there should be no advantage or disadvantage to holding dollars, German marks, the British pound sterling, and so on.[1]

However, serious balance of trade problems arose in the United States in the 1960s when the value of imports, including oil, began to greatly exceed exports. This meant foreign countries had an excess of dollars, which they could redeem in the United States for gold. By 1968 the demand for United States gold by foreign governments was very strong. Gold was worth much more on the open market than the nominal value of $35 an ounce at which the U.S. government was valuing it. The United States found itself in danger of losing its supply of gold. As a result, the U.S. and most other

---

1. As a country, the United States was on a gold standard from 1879-1971. The U.S. gold standard was modified slightly in 1934 when the government prohibited individuals from exchanging paper money for gold, or using gold as a medium of exchange. All new gold produced in the United States also had to be sold to the government. Restrictions on individual ownership of gold were removed when the United States went off the gold standard in 1971.

Western countries agreed to go off the gold standard in 1971 and to let their currencies float (have rates of exchange be set by market conditions) against each other.[2] Gold isn't used as a medium of exchange today because its bullion value is much greater than its face value. The dollar value of gold also fluctuates daily, adjusting to supply and demand for the metal and world wide economic conditions.

Strong and Weak Dollars

The terms *strong* and *weak* dollar are commonly used in the *Wall Street Journal* and other business publications with the assumption the reader knows what they mean. However, not all readers understand these terms, and their meanings aren't obvious. For example, a strong dollar, which sounds desirable, actually hurts U.S. exports. On the other hand, a weak dollar, which sounds undesirable, helps exports. Exhibits 10.1 shows how exchange rates affect the competitiveness of a U.S. company's products vis-a-vis a Japanese competitor.

In the first situation, where there are Y250 to the dollar, it is advantageous for a U.S. firm to buy the Japanese product. In the third situation, the opposite holds true. It is now advantageous for a U.S. firm to buy the American product. Somewhere in between there should be no difference in value.[3]

Assume a U.S. firm wants to buy a piece of earth moving equipment which costs $100,000 if made and sold in the U.S., or the Japanese equivalent made and sold in Japan.

Three sample situations are illustrated from the point of view of purchasers in the U.S. This is the point sometimes referred to as the *level playing field*, where theoretically U.S. and foreign products would compete only on their merits, not on an artificial advantage gained due to unusually high or low exchange rates.

The rising value of the dollar versus the yen in the early 1980s caused Caterpillar to lose significant market share in the earth moving equipment industry and lay off workers in the United States. Komatsu could make equipment in Japan and sell it for substantially less in the United States than Caterpillar could make and sell equivalent equipment in the United States, even in Caterpillar's home town of Peoria, Illinois. Caterpillar equipment made in Europe could also be imported into the United States and sold on the "gray market" (i.e., without manufacturer's warranty) for less than equivalent equipment made and sold in the United States. Not surprisingly, Caterpillar management was outspoken in its criticism of the strong dollar policy of the U.S. government in the early 1980s.[4]

---

2. Note that most Soviet block countries were not included. Trade with these countries was done in kind, meaning, for example, that the U.S. might send computers or machine tools to the Soviet Union in return for raw materials, such as oil. This occurs because the ruble is worth much less than its official exchange rate with the dollar. Thus if a U.S. manufacturer of computers sold a computer to the Soviet Union and was paid in rubles, the manufacturer couldn't get nearly the official exchange rate for the rubles if it wanted to buy something in the U.S. or other Western countries such as England, France or Germany.

3. This assumes no shipping charges, which can be significant in the case of heavy industrial equipment, and no import or export duties.

4. For example, see Carol J. Loomis, "How Companies are Coping with the Strong Dollar," *Fortune* , November 26, 1984, pp. 116-120; 122;124.

In the United States	In Japan	Comment
Situation 1: 250 yen/dollar (strong dollar)		
$100,000	converts to 25,000,000 yen	Advantageous to buy
	20,000,000 yen (cost in Japan)	Japanese product
	5,000,000 yen left over	
Situation 2: 200 yen/dollar (neutral dollar)		
$100,000	converts to 20,000,000 yen	No advantage to buy-
	20,000,000 yen (cost in Japan)	ing either product
	–0– yen left over	
Situation 3: 150 yen/dollar (weak dollar)		
$100,000	converts to 15,000,000 yen	Advantageous to buy
	20,000,000 yen (cost in Japan)	U.S. product
	(5,000,000) yen short	

Assumptions
1. If the machine is made and sold in the United States, its price in the United States remains the same regardless of the exchange rate (e.g., $100,000 for the piece of earth moving equipment).
2. If the machine is made and sold in Japan, its price in Japan remains the same regardless of the exchange rate (e.g., 20,000,000 yen for the equivalent piece of earth moving equipment).
3. The U.S. and Japanese pieces of equipment can be considered equivalent in quality and function.

Exhibit 10.1. Example of how fluctuations in exchange rates can affect the competitiveness of a U.S. company's product.

Undervalued and Overvalued Currencies

These concepts can be understood by considering the price of an item assumed to be the same throughout the world, such as a McDonald's Big Mac hamburger. Assume for purposes of demonstration that a Big Mac costs $2.20 in the U.S. and 4.30 Deutchmarks in Germany. Thus a person in the U.S. with $2.20 could buy a Big Mac. So too could a person in Germany with D4.30.

So far, so good. Now consider this situation. A person travelling to Germany and converting U.S. dollars into Deutchmarks would need to get D1.96 for each dollar to be able to buy a Big Mac in Germany in German currency (D1.96 * $2.20 = d4.30). If the official exchange rate is only D1.6/$, then the dollar is undervalued with respect to the deutchmark. A person travelling from Germany to the United States and converting deutchmarks into dollars would have the opposite experience. The D4.30 it costs to buy a Big Mac in Germany could be converted into $2.69, enough to buy a Big Mac in the United States for $2.20 and have $.49 in change. If the exchange rate changed so it was now D1.96/$, then the currencies would be said to trade at parity, meaning they had equal purchasing power in either country.

To summarize:

- The dollar is *undervalued*, or weak, with respect to another country's currency if it takes more dollars to buy the equivalent item in that country than it does in the United States.

■ The dollar is *overvalued*, or strong, with respect to another country's currency if it takes fewer dollars to buy the equivalent item in that country than it does in the United States.

■ The dollar is at *parity* if it takes the same number of dollars to buy the equivalent item in the United States or in another country.

The price of a Big Mac was used for demonstration purposes only. In practice, economists use sophisticated methods of measurement to determine whether one currency is over or undervalued with respect to another, but the principles are the same. Exhibit 10.2 shows some important effects of a strong and weak dollar on business.

	Favorable effects	Unfavorable effects
Strong dollar	Imported goods less expensive in U.S.	U.S. made goods more expensive in other countries. Bad for U.S. exports.
	Inexpensive to travel abroad.	Expensive to visit the U.S. (bad for the U.S. tourist industry)
	U.S. can make investments in other countries (including real estate and stocks) at bargain prices.	
Weak dollar	Imported goods more expensive in U.S.	U.S. made goods less expensive in other countries. Good for U.S. exports.
	Inexpensive to travel to the U.S. (good for the U.S. tourist industry)	
		Other countries can make investments in U.S. (including real estate and stock of U.S. firms) at bargain prices.

Exhibit 10.2. Effects of a strong and weak dollar on U.S. businesses.

SOME EFFECTS OF EXCHANGE RATE FLUCTUATIONS

Corporations doing a significant amount of business abroad need to pay close attention to the impact fluctuations in exchange rates can have on their profitability.

Location of R&D Facilities

With a strong dollar, U.S. firms have an incentive to locate their R&D facilities abroad, with a consequent loss of jobs in the U.S. With a weak dollar, foreign firms have an incentive to locate R&D facilities in the U.S., thus bringing jobs to the U.S. To balance out the potential adverse impact of exchange rate fluctuations, some large corporations choose to locate some of their facilities in the U.S. and some abroad. Thus they will be protected somewhat regardless of how exchange rates fluctuate.

Impact on the Manager of International Operations

International operations are now a major portion of many U.S. firms. Here's how the general manager of the international division of a major pharmaceutical firm described the problems caused by exchange rates.

My biggest problem in managing international operations was dealing with changes in exchange rates. Consider the effect on profits of a Japanese subsidiary when the dollar is getting stronger. The Japanese subsidiary can be performing very well when measured in yen.

But when those yen are converted in to dollars, the subsidiary's performance doesn't look so good. From my point of view, they need to reduce costs to improve profits as measured in dollars. From the local manager's point of view, his unit has done very well, growing perhaps twenty percent a year, and should be commended rather than asked to cut costs.

Of course, the situation is just the opposite when the dollar is weak. I looked like a genius in the mid-1980s when the value of the dollar fell to about 125 yen. Yet the performance of the overseas divisions as measured in local currencies hadn't changed very much.

To put this in quantitative terms, consider the impact on profits brought back to the United States from Japan if the dollar rises twenty percent against the yen (say from 100 to 120 yen per dollar). Now earnings must also rise twenty percent in yen if earnings are to remain the same when converted into dollars at the new rate of exchange. This effect can be so severe in countries with high rates of inflation that some United States companies may choose not to do business there.

SUMMARY

The general manager needs to know enough about exchange rates to realize the great impact they can have on a firm's financial performance. A strong dollar and a weak dollar each has its advantages and disadvantages. A strong dollar may cause the loss of American jobs because it is less expensive to buy equipment made abroad than to buy equivalent equipment made in the United States. However, a strong dollar also makes travel abroad less expensive and reduces the cost of investing in corporations or real estate abroad. The effects of a weak dollar, which existed in 1995 when this book was written, are just the opposite.

This has been a book about what the general manager should know about accounting and finance. It has been emphasized that the general manager should primarily be a *consumer* of financial and accounting information, not a *preparer* of it. While the basic objectives and concepts of accounting and finance stay the same, the rules or methods of implementation may change. This is primarily done through statements issued by the Financial Accounting Standards Board (FASB), whose purpose is to establish or improve standards of financial accounting and reporting.[1] While these statements are often technical in nature and difficult even for those with degrees in accounting to understand, more readable versions are usually available that have been prepared by one or more of the large public accounting firms for use by their clients.

The laws affecting accounting and financial practices may also change, especially with respect to taxes. This has been particularly true in the decade of the 1980s. The Economic Recovery Tax Act of 1981 implemented the Accelerated Cost Recovery System (ACRS) which contained significant changes in the methods of depreciation that could be used. Only five years later the Tax Reform Act of 1986 was passed, which made even more changes, particularly in tax rates. For the first time, the top individual tax rate of 28% was less than the top corporate rate of 34%. In 1993, the Omnibus Budget Reconciliation Act again made significant changes in the tax laws. The top marginal corporate tax rate rose to 35% for corporations with taxable income in excess of $10 million. The top personal tax rate rose to 35% for joint filers with taxable income over $140,000. A 10% surtax was also applied to taxable income over $250,000, creating an effective top rate of 39.6%. Thus individual rates could once again be higher than corporate tax rates.

Recognizing that changes in tax rates and in the application of accounting principles will occur from time to time, this book has concentrated on explaining the basic concepts of accounting and finance rather than demonstrating the application of current rules or procedures. Those can be found through current Internal Revenue Service publications available at any IRS office and often in the Reference Section of public libraries.

Since not all general managers have a degree in business (much less a major in accounting or finance), what is the least a general manager should know about accounting and finance? As a minimum, he or she should be able to read and understand the balance sheet and income statement included in an annual report. This includes being able to answer the following questions with confidence on the basis of his or her own analysis of the financial statements:

---

1. In the 1934 the Securities and Exchange Commission (SEC) was given the authority by federal law to prescribe financial accounting and reporting practices. However, the SEC delegated a major portion of this responsibility to the accounting profession. Since 1973 the FASB has had sole authority over the content and substance of its statements.

1. Can the company pay its bills?
2. Has the company borrowed too much money?
3. How well does the company make money?

Beyond this, he should know enough to ask pertinent questions of the experts he deals with in accounting and finance on such matters as the risks of leverage, the uses of break-even analysis, or the advantages of accelerated depreciation.

Many general mangers may also find it to their advantage to know something about two topics not covered in this book, cost accounting and inventory control. Managers in manufacturing businesses in particular should know the fundamentals of cost accounting. Since selling price is often kept down by competition, an individual firm's profitability is closely related to how well it controls costs in making its own products. Inventory is also very important in wholesaling and retailing businesses, where holding costs may run 25% or more of the value of inventory per year. Cost accounting systems are also very useful in such service businesses as advertising agencies and consulting firms, which should use them when bidding on jobs. No business can survive for long if it consistently bids jobs lower than the cost to complete them.

In conclusion, I will consider this book a success if it has removed any fear you might have had about reading financial statements. You should now know enough not only to be able to assess a firm's financial health, but also to "push the numbers" as necessary to find out where a firm makes its money or where its break-even point occurs. You free yourself from undue (and sometimes dangerous) reliance on accountants by developing confidence in your own ability to understand and analyze a balance sheet and an income statement. A solid grounding in the basic concepts of accounting and finance will always be an invaluable asset to you in your role as general manager.

Further Reading

Introductory Accounting

Dixon, Robert L., and Harold E. Arnett, *The McGraw-Hill 36-Hour Accounting Course*, third edition. New York: McGraw-Hill, 1993

Finance

Van Horne, James, *Fundamentals of Financial Management,* ninth edition. Englewood Cliffs, N.J.: Prentice Hall, 1995.

Financial Analysis

Bernstein, Leopold, *Financial Statement Analysis: Theory, Application and Interpretation*, fifth edition. Homewood, IL: Richard D. Irwin, 1992.

Droms, William G., *Finance and Accounting for Nonfinancial Managers*, third edition. Reading, MA: Addison-Wesley Publishing Company, 1990.

Fraser, Lyn M., *Understanding Financial Statements*, fourth edition. Englewood Cliffs, NJ: Prentice Hall, 1995.

Gibson, Charles H., *Financial Statement Analysis: Using Financial Accounting Information,* Cincinnati, OH: South-western, 1994.

Helfert, Eric A., *Techniques of Financial Analysis*. Homewood, IL: Irwin Professional Publishing, 1993.

Spiro, Herbert T., *Finance for the Nonfinancial Manager*, third edition. New York: John Wiley & Sons, 1988.

Tracy, John A., *How to Read a Financial Report: Wringing Cash Flows and Other Vital Signs Out of the Numbers*, fourth edition. New York: John Wiley & Sons, 1993.

Financial Data

Levine, Sumner, and Caroline Levine, editors, *The Business One Irwin Business & Investment Almanac*. Homewood, IL: Richard D. Irwin, published annually.

Ratio Analysis

Gates, Sheldon, *101 Business Ratios*. Scottsdale, AZ: McLane Publications, 1993.

IRS Publications

Selected IRS publications are listed below. Copies can usually be obtained from a local IRS office. IRS publications are also available in the Reference section of most public libraries. A full list of IRS publications can be found in the IRS Publication, *Guide to Free Tax Services.*

These and other IRS publications can be ordered free of charge from the IRS by calling the IRS toll-free at 1-800-829-3676.

Appendix A

Financial Analysis Forms

The following pages contain blank copies of forms which may be used to facilitate free cash flow analysis, ratio analysis and contribution analysis. Permission is hereby granted by the author for the purchaser of this book to reproduce and use these forms as necessary for his or her own personal use, including classes in which this book may be an assigned text. The author's permission must be obtained for any other use of these forms.

FREE CASH FLOW ANALYSIS

Company _____

Free cash flow is defined as cash flow (net income plus depreciation) minus dividends and minus capital spending.

To find a firm's free cash flow, refer to its **Value Line** sheet and complete the following:

	19__	19__	19__	19__
Cash flow/share	_____	_____	_____	_____
– Dividends/share	_____	_____	_____	_____
–Capital spending/share	_____	_____	_____	_____
= Free cash flow/share	_____	_____	_____	_____
x Shares outstanding	_____	_____	_____	_____
= Free cash flow	_____	_____	_____	_____

Total free cash flow for years given = $_____

COMMON FINANCIAL RATIOS

Company _____

			Years	
RATIO (Standard)		Formula	19___	19___
Current Ratio (1.5 : 1)	=	$\dfrac{\text{Current Assets}}{\text{Current Liabilities}}$	_____	_____
Liquidity Ratio (0.5 : 1)	=	$\dfrac{\text{Liquid Current Assets}}{\text{Current Liabilities}}$	_____	_____
Receivables (30 days)	=	$\dfrac{\text{Accounts Receivable}}{\text{Sales}} \times 360$	_____	_____
Payables (30 days)	=	$\dfrac{\text{Accounts Payable}}{\text{Cost of Goods Sold}} \times 360$	_____	_____
Inventory (days) (30 - 60 days)	=	$\dfrac{\text{Inventory}}{\text{Cost of Goods Sold}} \times 360$	_____	_____
Debt/Equity (< .5)	=	$\dfrac{\text{Long Term Debt}}{\text{Shareholders' Equity}}$	_____	_____
Assets/Sales (1 : 1 average)	=	$\dfrac{\text{Total Tangible Assets}}{\text{Sales}}$	_____	_____
Return on Sales (3 - 5% ave.)	=	$\dfrac{\text{Net Income}}{\text{Sales}}$	_____	_____
Return on Equity (15% minimum)	=	$\dfrac{\text{Net Income}}{\text{Shareholders' Equity}}$	_____	_____

ASSESSING A COMPANY'S FINANCIAL HEALTH

A.   Three basic questions:

1.   Can it pay its bills?   ___ Yes   ___ No

Current Ratio   = $\dfrac{\text{Current Assets}}{\text{Current Liabilities}}$ =   ____
(Good: 1.5 : 1)

Liquidity Ratio   = $\dfrac{\text{Liquid Current Assets}}{\text{Current Liabilities}}$ =   ____
(Good: 0.5: 1)

2.   Has it borrowed too much money?   ___ No   ___ Maybe   ___ Yes
                                                          < .5   .5 –1.0   > 1.0

Debt/Equity   = $\dfrac{\text{Long Term Debt}}{\text{Shareholders' Equity}}$ =   ____

3.   How well does it earn money?   ___ Very   ___Well   ___OK   ___Poor
                                                       Well
                                                   > 20%   15–20%   10–15%   < 10%

Return on Equity (%)   = $\dfrac{\text{Net Income} \times 100}{\text{Shareholders' Equity}}$ =   ____ %

B.   Overall assessment   ____ Excellent   ____ Good   ____ Fair   ____ Weak
of financial health

C.   Any special factors that should be noted about this firm:

_____

_____

_____

Contribution Analysis (in %)

Company _____

| Year | Segment/Region | | | | | | | Totals | |
	Sales	Pre-tax	Sales	Pre-tax	Sales	Pre-tax		Sales	Pre-tax
19___	_____	_____	_____	_____	_____	_____		100%	100%
19___	_____	_____	_____	_____	_____	_____		100%	100%
19___	_____	_____	_____	_____	_____	_____		100%	100%
19___	_____	_____	_____	_____	_____	_____		100%	100%

Appendix B

Goodwill and Deferred Pension Costs

This appendix covers two entries that do not always appear on the balance sheet, but which can be quite large when they do appear.

The Goodwill Entry

Goodwill is defined as the excess of purchase price over fair market value of an asset or business. It is a "plug number" to balance the fundamental equation of accounting: Assets = Liabilities + Shareholders' equity. Thus if a small business's assets were appraised at $250,000 and the business was sold for $300,000, the difference of $50,000 would be shown as goodwill on the asset side of the acquiring firm's balance sheet. Goodwill has no value. From the accountant's point of view the acquirer has exchanged $50,000 of cash for $50,000 of goodwill.

Until 1993, goodwill could not be deducted for tax purposes the way depreciation was. Starting in 1993, the U.S. Tax Code was changed to permit certain intangibles, including goodwill, to be deducted as an expense (amortized) *before* computing taxes, just the way depreciation was deducted. Eligible intangibles must now be amortized over fifteen years using a straightline basis. For financial reporting (e.g., statements in annual reports), companies may amortize intangibles using a straightline basis over a period not to exceed forty years.

The expression for cash flow developed in Chapter 2 now becomes:

Cash flow = Net income + Depreciation of assets

+ Amortization of intangibles

+ Change in deferred taxes.

Amortization of intangibles becomes a component of cash flow because, like depreciation, it is a non-cash charge against earnings. In Chapter 2 we saw how deferred taxes can arise when accelerated depreciation is used to compute taxes and straightline depreciation is used to compute earnings. The same effect occurs when intangibles are amortized for a different period of time for tax purposes than for financial reporting.

If goodwill is small, the effect on earnings in negligible. But goodwill can be very large. When Philip Morris acquired Kraft for $12.9 billion in cash in 1988, accountants valued Kraft's assets at only $1.3 billion, leaving the remaining $11.6 billion to be accounted for as goodwill. The $11.6 billion of goodwill was more than Philip Morris's 1988 net worth of $7.7 billion. If it had all been charged against earnings in one year, Philip Morris would have had a *negative* net worth of over three billion dollars. Yet Philip Morris is a highly profitable firm and the acquisition of Kraft was viewed favorably by investors. No wonder there is so much concern about the treatment of goodwill.[1]

When firms have large intangible assets, the largest component by far is usually goodwill associated with acquisition of other firms. Here are some acquisitions where a very large amount of goodwill was involved:

1988	Philip Morris's acquisition of Kraft	$11.6 billion
1988	Kodak's acquisition of Sterling Drug	$5.0 billion
1993	Merck's acquisition of Medco	$5.1 billion
1994	Lilly's acquisition of PCS	$4.1 billion
1995	Quaker Oat's acquisition of Snapple	$750 million

Is a large amount of goodwill necessarily bad? Not necessarily. Future earning ability is what is really important in the market. When Philip Morris acquired Kraft, shareholders clearly approved, as its stock appreciated more than 50% in the next year. On the other hand, shareholders weren't so enthusiastic when Quaker Oats acquired Snapple, the health food beverage firm. The price of Quaker Oats stock fell nearly 50% in the next year.

The Deferred Pension Cost Entry

This entry is similar in concept to goodwill in that it is a plug number to preserve the fundamental equation of accounting. It is listed on the asset side of the balance sheet just like goodwill. The entry arises when a firm's contributions to its pension fund are less than its anticipated pension fund liabilities in future years.

The amount of underfunding should be deducted from shareholders' equity to give a more accurate value of the firm's net worth. If the underfunding is significant, it could reduce the firm's equity base significantly. Thus accountants permit the deferred pension cost to be amortized over a period of years just like goodwill.

SUMMARY

The computation of goodwill and deferred pension costs should be left to the accountants. However, the general manager should be able to recognize these entries when they do occur on the balance sheet, know why they occur, and know how they can be the source of significant adjustments to net worth. Most firms won't have either of these entries on their balance sheets.

Significant amounts of goodwill usually arise only when a consumer products firm (such as Kraft) or a service firm (such as a radio station) is acquired where the value of the physical assets is a small portion of the purchase price. Deferred pension costs represent a situation where pension liabilities have been underfunded. Generally this happens only when a firm starts a pension plan (and must make provision for employees' prior service) or is so short of cash from operations it can't ade-

---

1. See Jeffery M. Laderman, "Goodwill is Making a Lot of People Angry," *Business Week*, July 31, 1989, pp.73-74.

quately fund its pension plan each year (like a steel firm in the 1980s). If a firm has adequately funded its pension plan, there should be no entry for deferred pension costs.

APPENDIX C

Present Value of $1

Future Years	1%	2%	4%	6%	8%	10%	12%	14%	15%	16%	18%	20%	22%	24%	25%	26%	28%	30%	35%	40%	45%	50%
1	.990	.980	.962	.943	.926	.909	.893	.877	.870	.862	.847	.833	.820	.806	.800	.794	.781	.769	.741	.714	.690	.667
2	.980	.961	.925	.890	.857	.826	.797	.769	.756	.743	.718	.694	.672	.650	.640	.630	.610	.592	.549	.510	.476	.444
3	.971	.942	.889	.840	.794	.751	.712	.675	.658	.641	.609	.579	.551	.524	.512	.500	.477	.455	.406	.364	.328	.296
4	.961	.924	.855	.792	.735	.683	.636	.592	.572	.552	.516	.482	.451	.423	.410	.397	.373	.350	.301	.260	.226	.198
5	.951	.906	.822	.747	.681	.621	.567	.519	.497	.476	.437	.402	.370	.341	.328	.315	.291	.269	.223	.186	.156	.132
6	.942	.888	.790	.705	.630	.564	.507	.456	.432	.410	.370	.335	.303	.275	.262	.250	.227	.207	.165	.133	.108	.088
7	.933	.871	.760	.665	.583	.513	.452	.400	.376	.354	.314	.279	.249	.222	.210	.198	.178	.159	.122	.095	.074	.059
8	.923	.853	.731	.627	.540	.467	.404	.351	.327	.305	.266	.233	.204	.179	.168	.157	.139	.123	.091	.068	.051	.039
9	.914	.837	.703	.592	.500	.424	.361	.308	.284	.263	.225	.194	.167	.144	.134	.125	.108	.094	.067	.048	.035	.028
10	.905	.820	.676	.558	.463	.386	.322	.270	.247	.227	.191	.162	.137	.116	.107	.099	.085	.073	.050	.035	.024	.017
11	.896	.804	.650	.527	.429	.350	.287	.237	.215	.195	.162	.135	.112	.094	.086	.079	.066	.056	.037	.025	.017	.012
12	.887	.788	.625	.497	.397	.319	.257	.208	.187	.168	.137	.112	.092	.076	.069	.062	.052	.043	.027	.018	.012	.008
13	.879	.773	.601	.469	.368	.290	.229	.182	.163	.145	.116	.093	.075	.061	.055	.050	.040	.033	.020	.013	.008	.005
14	.870	.758	.577	.442	.340	.263	.205	.160	.141	.125	.099	.078	.062	.049	.044	.039	.032	.025	.015	.009	.006	.003
15	.861	.743	.555	.417	.315	.239	.183	.140	.123	.108	.084	.065	.051	.040	.035	.031	.025	.020	.011	.006	.004	.002
16	.853	.728	.534	.394	.292	.218	.163	.123	.107	.093	.071	.054	.042	.032	.028	.025	.019	.015	.008	.005	.003	.002
17	.844	.714	.513	.371	.270	.198	.146	.108	.093	.080	.060	.045	.034	.026	.023	.020	.015	.012	.006	.003	.002	.001
18	.836	.700	.494	.350	.250	.180	.130	.095	.081	.069	.051	.038	.028	.021	.018	.016	.012	.009	.005	.002	.001	.001
19	.828	.686	.475	.331	.232	.164	.116	.083	.070	.060	.043	.031	.023	.017	.014	.012	.009	.007	.003	.002	.001	
20	.820	.673	.456	.312	.215	.149	.104	.073	.061	.051	.037	.026	.019	.014	.012	.010	.007	.005	.002	.001	.001	
25	.780	.610	.375	.233	.146	.092	.059	.038	.030	.024	.016	.010	.007	.005	.004	.003	.002	.001	.001			
30	.742	.552	.308	.174	.099	.057	.033	.020	.015	.012	.007	.004	.003	.002	.001	.001		.001				
40	.672	.453	.208	.097	.048	.022	.011	.005	.004	.003	.001							.001				

APPENDIX D

Present Value of $1 Received for Each of the Next N Years

Years	2%	4%	6%	8%	10%	12%	14%	15%	16%	18%
1	.980	.962	.943	.926	.909	.893	.877	.870	.862	.847
2	1.942	1.886	1.833	1.783	1.736	1.690	1.647	1.626	1.605	1.566
3	2.884	2.775	2.673	2.577	2.487	2.402	2.322	2.283	2.246	2.174
4	3.808	3.630	3.465	3.312	3.170	3.037	2.914	2.855	2.798	2.690
5	4.713	4.452	4.212	3.993	3.791	3.605	3.433	3.352	3.274	3.127
6	5.601	5.242	4.917	4.623	4.355	4.111	3.889	3.784	3.685	3.498
7	6.472	6.002	5.582	5.206	4.868	4.564	4.228	4.160	4.039	3.812
8	7.325	6.733	6.210	5.747	5.335	4.968	4.639	4.487	4.344	4.078
9	8.163	7.435	6.802	6.247	5.759	5.328	4.946	4.772	4.607	4.303
10	8.983	8.111	7.360	6.710	6.145	5.650	5.216	5.019	4.833	4.494

Years	20%	22%	24%	25%	26%	28%	30%	35%	40%	50%
1	.833	.820	.806	.800	.794	.781	.769	.741	.714	.667
2	1.528	1.492	1.457	1.440	1.424	1.392	1.361	1.289	1.224	1.111
3	2.106	2.042	1.981	1.952	1.923	1.868	1.816	1.696	1.589	1.407
4	2.589	2.494	2.404	2.362	2.320	2.241	2.166	1.997	1.849	1.605
5	2.991	2.864	2.745	2.689	2.635	2.532	2.436	2.220	2.035	1.737
6	3.326	3.167	3.020	2.951	2.885	2.759	2.643	2.385	2.168	1.824
7	3.605	3.416	3.242	3.161	3.083	2.937	2.802	2.508	2.263	1.883
8	3.837	3.619	3.421	3.329	3.241	3.076	2.925	2.598	2.331	1.922
9	4.031	3.786	3.566	3.463	3.366	3.184	3.019	2.665	2.379	1.948
10	4.192	3.923	3.682	3.571	3.465	3.269	3.092	2.715	2.414	1.965

INDEX